IFA

The Yoruba God of Divination in Nigeria and the United States

Louis Djisovi Ikukomi Eason

With Reflections and Commentaries Edited by

Toyin Falola

Africa World Press, Inc.

P.O. Box 1892
Trenton, NJ 08607

P.O. Box 48
Asmara, ERITREA

Africa World Press, Inc.

P.O. Box 1892
Trenton, NJ 08607

P.O. Box 48
Asmara, ERITREA

Copyright © 2008 Louis Djisovi Ikukomi Eason
First Printing 2008

All rights reserved. No part of this publication may be reproduced, stored in a retrieval system or transmitted in any form or by any means electronic, mechanical, photocopying, recording or otherwise without the prior written permission of the publisher.

Book and cover design: Saverance Publishing Services
(www.saverancepublishing.com)

Cover Photos (left to right):
   Writer's Altar Room with Ifa sacred artifacts at the Center.
   Festival Participants from the Ifa Pilgrimage entering the Ifa Temple, Ile Ife, 1992
   The Asheda (Ile Ife) with Tosu in Ifa ceremony preparing Egungun Masks for performance at Bowling Green State University, 1993

Library of Congress Cataloging-in-Publication Data

Eason, Louis Djisovi Ikukomi, 1949-2005.
  Ifa : the Yoruba god of divination in Nigeria and the United States / Louis Djisovi Ikukomi Eason ; with reflections and commentaries edited by Toyin Falola.
    p. cm.
  Includes bibliographical references.
  ISBN 1-59221-640-4 (hardcover) -- ISBN 1-59221-641-2 (pbk.)
  1. Ifa (Religion) 2. Divination--Nigeria. 3. Divination--United States. I. Falola, Toyin. II. Title.

BF1779.I4E37 2008
299.6'8333--dc22

                              2008032720

IFA

Table of Contents

PART A
REFLECTIONS AND COMMENTARIES

Reflections on Eason's Life and Work *Lillian Ashcraft-Eason*	ix
First Commentary: Accepting Destiny *Rev. Oloye Aina Olomo*	xix
Second Commentary: Eason on Ifa *Akinloye Ojo*	xxxi
Acknowledgements	li

PART B
THE TEXT

Chapter 1 *Memories and Observations on Ifa Religion and Culture in Ile-Ife and Oyotunji*	3
Chapter 2 *The Oduduwa Influence on Ifa*	37
Chapter 3 *Oyotunji: African Americans Recover Ifa*	73
Chapter 4 *The Ifa Festival At Ile-Ife*	109
Chapter 5 *"A Time of Destiny": Celebrating Ifa in Oyotunji*	139
Afterword	161
Photos	175
Appendix	181
Index	187

PART A

REFLECTIONS AND COMMENTARIES

Reflections on Eason's Life and Work

Lillian Ashcraft-Eason

In July and August of 2005, Djisovi began to say good-bye, but he looked good physically so I was in denial. The day that he had the cerebral hemorrhage began like every other morning—nothing extraordinary. I went to campus while he stayed at home to prepare a lecture for his afternoon class in African religions in the United States. His nephew called before he left for class to say that he and his wife were naming their son, who was born two days after Djisovi died, Gabriel Louis. Djisovi left after the phone call—about which his nephew later told me—and lectured on the Yoruba concept of *Iwapele* (good character); he told his students that he wanted to be remembered for having good character. He was stricken before he left the classroom.

Paralyzed in his right side, he dragged himself across campus and found me to say that he was having a stroke. I embraced him and went to get help. Remaining lucid and calm for about 25 minutes, he told doctors that he was in no pain. Making sure that I was beside his bed in the emergency room, he smiled slightly, closed his eyes, and slipped into a coma. The ER and Intensive Care staffs permitted neighbors and colleagues to visit, but five of us stayed in his room for long stretches of time. We sang to him Yoruba and Fon songs that he had taught us, and we prayed a prayer that we heard from his lips many times. In his wallet, he carried a printed copy of the Ifa prayer that he cited in Chapter 2. About 19 hours later, the medical staff pronounced him dead. That was on September 21—a little over a month after our 20th wedding anniversary; we had married on August 17, 1985 on Marcus Garvey's birthday. He was a faithful, attentive, affectionate, fun-loving husband, my closest friend.

One of my first impressions of him when we first met in January 1984 was that Djisovi was devoted to studying African Traditional Religions (ATR), especially those of the Yoruba and Fon. He had studied and lived them for more than a decade in 1984. Soon after we met, I asked him to teach me about Africa. He recommended a reading list. The first book was Harold W. Percival's *Thinking and Destiny*. Percival's thinking about rhythms of the universe, the human body, consciousness, and ultimate reality prepared me for cosmological perspectives in ATR. I read books as if preparing for an examination for about a year. Meanwhile Djisovi maneuvered to get me into audiences with Oba Oseijeman and Medahochi. Both loved to talk, had read broadly, and ably expounded on religion and Yoruba mytho-history. I credit Djisovi with taking me beyond western-oriented courses that I had studied on Africa for college credits; he coaxed me along to peer inside traditional Africa.

I never knew Djisovi as a practicing babalawo with clients. He had stopped accepting clients for divinations around 1980, while living in Gary. Partially he was impressed by something that Kpojito had said, "If folk will live righteously and stay attuned to their *ori*, they will need only occasional divinations." He admired Medahochi's penchant for indigenizing aspects of the Oyotunji Movement but was sometimes uncomfortable. Since he had not known Medahochi to be initiated to Ifa or Fa, Djisovi wondered if Medahochi had authority to conduct his 1979 Fa initiation. Not wanting to offend Medahochi or contribute to a rift that he perceived between Oba Oseijeman and Medahochi, Djisovi waited six years to approach Oseijeman for a corrective rite. The Ifa initiation in 1985 strengthened the bond between Oba Oseijeman and Djisovi; his respect for Medahochi as godfather and his support of Medahochi's endeavors endured. Djisovi's scholarly pursuit of Ifa and Fa continued.

When we first married, Djisovi told me that there would have to be Fon and/or Yoruba rites performed when he died. Because of Medahochi's declining health and Djisovi's fondness for him, I sent for his godbrother, Tosu. An organizing member of our Egungun society, he performed the private rites with aplomb and read a devotional Odu at the public memorial service. Tosu continued to guide me through the successive funerary rituals, undoubtedly with guidance from Medahochi. Oba Oseijeman had asked Djisovi and me to bring him whatever literature we found on funeralizing Yoruba kings. We brought materials to him and Medahochi.

Reared by his mother—along with two sisters and two brothers—and tutored in the rudiments of ritualizing the orishas and vodouns by the Kpojito, Djisovi appreciated strength in women. He thought they should complement their adopted, birth, or spiritual family members and have ability to be independently self-supporting. He wanted women to have spiritual vibrancy that impelled them to face challenges and voice their interests as they deem appropriate. He expected toughness and tenderness to be operative countervailing forces in women and especially in mothers, for our lives and social development—he would say on stage—begin with mother.

Impulses aside, Djisovi's studies led him to believe that women should be accorded more of a commanding role in the Ifa priesthood. He read books on Ifa in libraries in the United States and in Ile-Ife, and he bought books, was given booklets and essays, and accumulated useful references. The more that he read the more convinced Djisovi was that the Ifa priesthood was misguided in its male chauvinism. He cherished C. O. Osamaro Ibie's narrative on the role of the deity Arugba in the first establishment of Earth. He believed that after reading it, a fair-minded priest would rethink the chauvinistic perspective. Ebie's narrative on the first habitation of earth, which has excerpts in the Appendix, is informative though provocative about women's role in Creation.

The issue of whether women can be accepted into full membership in the Ifa priesthood continues unresolved. Meanwhile iyanifas, such as the Rev. Chief Iyanifa Fagbemileke Fatunmise (Faseun of Ile-Ife and Iyagan Agbaye—chief priestess of Eegun) in Atlanta, have received both hands of Ifa in West Africa. She and other progressive-minded women conclude from their studies that iyanifas innately have what babalawos call Odu (female energy) and do not need to see or be given it. The Rev. Chief Iyanifa believes that they have so much of that energy that if they see it in Odu, they will die.

Prior to receiving both hands of Ifa, the Rev. Chief Iyanifa used only cowry shells to divine. Now when she derives the Odu through merindologun divination, she casts the special Opele chain of babalawos over that Odu to see if she should also beat ikin. Having been initiated to Ifa in Ile-Ife, she accepts full authority to initiate others to this orisha when the occasion presents itself. She thinks, as Djisovi did, that Ifa priestesses may choose to be called iyalawo or iyanifa. Based on their initiative and constructive analysis of Ifa verses, women seem destined to claim authority within the Ifa priesthood for themselves.

Djisovi was a babalawo who supported women in their bid to be promoted within the Ifa priesthood. While we conducted research on Yoruba history and Ifa culture during the summer of 1992, Djisovi requested that he be taken through rites to receive both hands of Ifa while still in Ile-Ife. He was delighted that the Asheda beckoned for me to accompany Djisovi in receiving both hands of Ifa. Having already discerned that Djisovi had been initiated to Ifa and seen Odu, the Asheda offered a shortened ritual that could serve the dual purposes of giving Djisovi both hands and making me an iyanifa. The Asheda said that Djisovi and I were twins and should receive the 32 ikin plus *Oduso* (Eshu), and other pertinent objects together. When we returned home, Djisovi told his babalawo colleagues about our experience. He proudly observed my practicing with the ikin and often referred to me as iyalawo, despite my feeling awkward and being in awe of his considerable knowledge and longevity as a priest of Hevioso and a babalawo. Throughout the book, he has argued in support of the feminist cause in the Ifa priesthood.

Djisovi and I were simultaneously installed as chiefs in the Egungun society in Ile-Ife. In 1993, we were authorized to organize an extension of that society. Members there sent their representative, Chief Adebayo Ogundijo, to initiate us and assist us in organizing the society. Titles of *Atokun* and *Iya Ato*—male and female chiefs were bestowed upon us respectively. The Egungun cloth (*agan*) is kept by the Iya Ato, and she is the only female who may be present during preparations for Egungun ceremonies. Djisovi and I received articles of dress and other accoutrements symbolizing our offices with the initiation. He and I cherished these opportunities to formally pay homage to our ancestors and celebrate our twin spirits.

He and I were professional partners, consulting with each other on teaching, bolstering my specialty in African-American history and religion with his knowledge in culture studies and skills in African percussions. We team-taught and supported each other in research and development of academic programs. We jointly traveled to conferences and enrolled into Spanish and history of religion courses. About his fondness for our explorations in Paris, Djisovi had mixed emotions; he enjoyed touring cathedrals and museums, strolling along the *Champs Elysees* and stopping at popular tourist sites, but he wanted to feel that he had tempered that joy with meaningful analysis of French colonialism's legacy of underdevelopment in the Republic of Benin. When we took students to lunch or dinner in the Eiffel Tower, Djisovi wanted them to remember their soulful meals at Maman Benin's in Cotonou. The partnership necessitated bargaining and sensitivity amidst our explorations.

Curiosity and the desire to broaden our knowledge of Fon culture inspired us to study Vodou beyond the sensationalism of Hollywood. We knew as scholars that religion and language open the way to learning cultures. When we began taking students on a travel and study seminar in the Republic of Benin, we learned more about Vodou and Fon traditional culture. In addition to our forays into Vodou temples and ceremonies, we learned that there was a vodou entity in Cotonou that is called Thron Church. Despite their vivid memory and ritualizing of Nana Buluku and Mawu—Supreme Creators--and the relative altruism among various levels of priesthood, male chauvinism is pervasive. Although the question of whether Thron is a Vodoun lingers, patriarchal notions that persist among orisha worshippers are observable in this church that our seminar participants attend each summer.

Djisovi thought, as do some other New Yorubas, that he and I should participate in the Protestant religions of our African-American ancestors. We joined Methodist and Baptist churches and performed in pageants and took part in other programs. Pastors often welcomed our offers to teach about African traditional cultures and religions. These churches afforded us opportunities to learn, serve and teach.

Assessing his role as a New Yoruba, Djisovi said that his calling was to teach and perform repertoires from Yoruba and Fon Traditional Religions. Performance was a family matter for him. I sang traditional songs and danced with him on several occasions. He cajoled his three sons into performing in various capacities with him. He had passion for performing and teaching rhythms, songs, dances, and folktales to children in schools and churches. He used personal funds in that cause, bringing Traditionalists from Ile-Ife and New Yorubas from several parts of the United States to perform and teach Yoruba cultural arts.

At Bowling Green State University, he was appointed Coordinator of Ethnic Cultural Performing Arts. This position gave him the opportunity to organize an annual event—*Odun Omo Eniyan (first children of Human Being)*—as a culminating program for his work with children in Bowling Green-Toledo area schools and churches, having them perform what they learned from him during the year. As he returned to the schools or met the youth about the city during the year, they greeted him with songs or parts of folktales that they had heard during his interactive performances with them. About three months before he died we went out to breakfast and as we left the restaurant, the bus boy started singing one of the songs. Djisovi's continence glowed with appreciation.

Djisovi had a strong sense of history. Consequently, he preserved records from the early 1970s, and he photographed and videotaped most performances, programs, and field studies and travel-study seminars. When he was ready to write, helpful records were in his files; these sometimes guided him to other manuscript and printed documents and served as a check on his memory. He thought that he had something important to say in a book and was determined to re-write his dissertation for publication. To this end in 2003, he conducted research in the Melville Herskovits Collection at Northwestern University. He had a full draft by the end of summer 2004.

We spent much of the next year (2005) attending last rites of passage and mourning losses of loved ones. Several principals in his book died. Akanke (Nochi) transitioned in Milwaukee in January, Chief Adebayo Ogundijo in February in Ile-Ife, Nigeria, and Oba Oseijeman in Oyotunji African Village in February. We attended the two funerals in the U.S. and telephoned our condolences to the family in Nigeria. We took students to tour and study African

American culture in the Sea Islands and Oyotunji in March. In July, Djisovi and I traveled to Oyotunji for a third time that year for the coronation of the Oba's son. He video-taped those activities and rituals.

His youthful pan-Africanism matured into a mellow pan-humanism that won admiration and reward. While at Clark Atlanta University, Dr. Sylvia Walsh Perkins—a professor in the Department of Religion and Philosophy--successfully nominated him for a Michael Jackson Scholarship from the United Negro College Fund. Djisovi used a portion of those monies to cut a CD of African and African-American popular music with his philosophy professor (Dr. Ralph Ellis) and members of Tiyehimba-- Adebayo Bello (of Nigeria) and Richard Owens and David Chandler (of Atlanta). Djisovi and Bello had organized Tiyehimba as a performing group of musicians, and the group acquired recognition and success in Atlanta. To memorialize his contributions to the Academy and his pan-humanist stature Bowling Green State University established a scholarship in his honor. His godson, Seneca Vaught, wrote a chapter about Djisovi in his doctoral dissertation and completed a video documentary on aspects of his life.

While he touted his African ancestry, Djisovi acknowledged his Cherokee and German-Jewish heritages. Having learned about the African origins of *Homo sapiens* and about race as a social construction, he was comfortable with his mixed ancestry. He acquired an attitude of love for all people and believed that one should celebrate human life by interacting with those around him.

He daily took time to greet and chat with friends, colleagues, and those whom he met while walking through the neighborhood, traveling, and shopping. He often would remind me that one of his responsibilities was to show love to people with more than a casual, fleeting greeting, so he hugged them and lingered for a time to chat. Djisovi would say, "Academe is structured to keep professors and students so preoccupied with research and publishing, teaching and learning, attending meetings and writing reports that they have virtually no time to stop to chat. Well I am not going to live my life on campus with that kind of angst. I am going to take time to reach out and linger over a few words. I don't care what you or anybody else think I should be doing." I would smile and continue to meet colleagues and friends with a wave and nod while rushing on to the next chore—often leaving him behind to chat. He would not be deterred from interactive, casual fellowship. Djisovi was proud, nonetheless, of every word that he published. One accomplishment of which he was proudest was the published essay on contemporary African Traditional Religions that he and I wrote together for publication.

I am thankful that he showed interest in traditional Africa and had a pan-humanist embrace. I am fortunate that he loved and was affectionate. Now I am the recipient of appreciation from a vast network of those to whom he gave and meant much. I continue to study the African ancestral past and to honor his memory as I direct the Benin Seminar.

First Commentary
Accepting Destiny

Rev. Oloye Aina Olomo
Iyalorisa, Iya Agan, Iyalawo, the Ajidakin

It is my hope that I add a contextual perspective to this work because what has been documented is very close to what I encountered during my own journey. Although the author was both an established academician and a practitioner, I am a practitioner writing about a practitioner. Ifa Orisa people in the Western, so-called "New World," have important contributions to make to the Pan-Yoruba Diaspora. This work has significant value because it addresses many of the issues that have been encountered by Americans in pursuit of Ifa. Reading this book has been wonderful; it allowed me to revisit the road behind me.

This work is an important contribution to the global strides of Ifa traditions because it documents many of the initial motivations that ushered in a whole new epoch of African history in the "New World." It is a historical report of one man's journey back to the spirituality and culture of Yoruba ancestors. Members of our generation, his and mine, followed the paths blazed by many elders in the United States. This body of information recorded by Chief Dr. Djisovi Eason is a large footprint left in the sand, generously, for future generations, a testament to the ability and courage of those pathfinders who traveled this road before us. Many of our contemporaries stood on the sidelines and critically watched the first tentative strides African Americans took toward the reclamation and revitalization of African Spirituality. While some were critical and uninvolved, others were able to push aside their ego and engage the old ways that were new to our experience; Dr. Eason was certainly one who chose to take the way of the ancient ancestors.

Each chapter is a stepping stone that leads the reader on a circuitous path through the political issues of the time; the author stops briefly at critical junctions where decisions and adaptations had to be made. He allows us to eavesdrop on the conversations and epiphanies of the pathfinders. This gives the reader an opportunity to see the issues facing African Americans from the purview of an insider. He writes extensively about the early days of Oyotunji Village in Sheldon, South Carolina and its movement toward the reclamation of Ifa tradition. The untimely conclusion of this manuscript reflects one of the realities of the reclamation movement; those left behind are obligated to carry it forward. He provides valuable insight into the structure of the Ifa Festivals that are held annually in Ile-Ife, Nigeria and Oyotunji Village in the United States. The road he takes us down is not a one-way highway leading us straight to Ile-Ife; the route diverges and takes a brief detour into the beliefs and sacred traditions of the Fon of the Benin Republic. While there are global issues that connect people, there are also dogmatic attitudes and appli-

First Commentary: Accepting Destiny

cations that present differences of opinion—gender roles is one of those issues. He raises questions that point out the contradictions between the sacred text of Ifa and the cultural realities of men and women. At an important crossroad he comes into possession of a precious stone, the Ifa Festival of Ile-Ife.

The role of women in Ifa is a thread that runs through this book. Internationally, In general, Ifa communities pattern the assignment of gender roles similar to that of Christianity by encouraging each sex to do work that resembles the simplified gender-positions of the church's religious clergy. The Christian Church is an institution that views the Supreme Being and *His* most influential prophets as male. Dr. Eason questions the foresight of leaders and scholars concerning their interpretation of the work women do. The role of the female in many World Religions has been interpreted as *less* than that of the male and the functions or roles of the women within the religious body are socially and ritually classified as those of subordinates.

In Chapter One the author describes his first-hand experiences of the African American Church and his involvement in community affairs. Dr. Eason reports his early encounters with Georgia racism and his response — activism. Ultimately he was led to investigate the wholistic religious way of an Ifa lifestyle. He gives a detailed description of many of the elements of Ifa and how they permeate every aspect of individual and communal life. He was not unlike many seekers of African Spirituality during the sixties. Most of us refined our political views first and attempted to discard the effects that institutionalized racism had on our lives and on the lives of everyone we knew. Resistance of total enculturation was a critical component of what sent many people in search of a spirituality that was compatible with their evolving politics.

Not only was resistance critical, it is critical; as we move toward the universal purpose of *Ifa*, it is vital for the forward motion of humanity.

Historically, the retention of African traditional religion in the West has offered devotees a freedom that is the result of cultural grounding, and it has provided creative methodologies of expression and rituals that emancipated the spirit despite the cultural, economic, and intellectual challenges that had to be conquered. The main feature of this chapter is that the author is the first to take a comparative look at Ifa in Nigeria and the U.S. He documents what developed out of the struggle of those who went in search of Afro-centric politics and arrived at spirituality. He makes a useful comparison between the two related systems uniquely African in Oyotunji beside the cornerstone of Ifa worship, Ile-Ife.

In Chapter Two, Dr. Eason takes a closer look at the mythology of Ile-Ife. He has a childlike innocence and awe that draws the reader into a divine web of deities, ghosts, and magic associated with the locale. He asserts that the myths and history of Ile-Ife are important to all Yoruba because it is where life began. He gives the reader valid questions to consider when he asks whether or not today's Ife is the same Ife of ancient times. He offers seven different considerations as the actual location of Ile-Ife, the origins of many of the Orisa in Nigeria can be traced to historical personalities and specific locales. Discussion of Ile-Ife leads us to many of the histories surrounding the progenitors of the Yoruba—Oduduwa and the aboriginal deity Obatala.

First Commentary: Accepting Destiny

The second part of Chapter Two examines the question "What is Ifa?" He discusses the force of energy that gets things done, *ase*. The realm of *ase* or mystery (*awo*) is a world without boundaries, constantly regenerating, expanding its breadth and depth; this is the dimension of consciousness where the sum total of humanity's inspirations and experiences are alive, existing forever in the minutes of today never solely attentive or restricted to yesterday or tomorrow.

I agree with Dr. Eason that *ase* is practical and capable of immediate access by Ifa diviners. This power brings everything in the Universe into existence. Its apparatus is dialectical, creating harmony-dysfunction, joy-sadness, awareness-unconsciousness, and matter-thought, light-darkness, as they co-exist in the consciousness of Source simultaneously. *Awo* and *ase* are the space in the universe where the illusive answer to *how* dwells. Keeping up with the worldwide scope and destiny of Ifa is no easy task. The author describes the method of divination and makes it easy to understand what people see when the diviner manipulates the sacred palm nuts, the *ikin*.

One of the most interesting aspects of Chapter Two is what the author reports about the gender polarization within the hierarchy of Ifa. He advises the reader that the divine feminine principle was probably inherited by the pre-Oduduwa era or the indigenous Igbo people. He ascertains that the Igbo people were more mother-centered before Yoruba civilization moved into an era of the feminization of poverty and the masculization of power.

It is not strange to me that Dr. Eason, as an Ifa practitioner and scholar of the reclamation movement, is prompted to question how his colleagues avoid or miss the limitations placed on women by Ifa leaders. In the Diaspora, women have been an integral part in the building of social and religious capital. We have been the keepers and dispensers of ethical, moral, and spiritual identities. As productive beings, women are a form of social capital; we are assets who are available for use in the production of further assets.

The faithful of Ifa traditions have built their identities around gender roles that do not support male and female balance, is an essential characteristic of Ifa theology. In building these identities, male devotees have had to learn to carry the burden of interpreting theological policies without adding the perspective, assistance, and understanding of women; and the women within our spiritual communities have learned that they have no voice in setting the theological standards by which they are expected to live.

Right now, in the United States there are more Iyanifas, women initiated into the priesthood of Ifa, than have been recorded as being seen in Nigeria. It must not be lost that it has been the Mothers of Yoruba-based spiritual traditions that have held on tightly to their memories and developed ways to practice in hostile environments. Among Yoruba practitioners in the West, generations of Maes (Mothers) of the Orixa in Brazil's Candomble have kept the tradition going through hundreds of years of slavery and colonization. The spiritual Mothers of Trinidad have been the stronghold and the majority of the caretakers for Sango Orisa traditions.

Dr. Eason cites the oracle of Osa Meji to explain the power given to women by the Supreme Being, making her the chief of all divinities. Osa Meji says to everyone that there is a need to respect the position and power given to women. It says, *"Prostrate, prostrate for the women. Woman has placed you in the world, thus you are of humanity. Woman is the intelligence of the*

First Commentary: Accepting Destiny

earth, prostrate for women. Woman has placed you in the world, thus you are of humanity."

Within the constructs of developing gender identity, freedom is approached; with the application of self-determination comes self-identification.

Chapter Three takes a close look at the establishment of Oyotunji Village and its founder. He describes the history and the culture in the area surrounding the Village. There were active remnants of Africanisms in the sea-islands near Oyotunji. Acknowledgment of these African retentions brings Dr. Eason back to the African-American Church. He concludes that the spiritual and cultural patterns of West Africa were not consciously "lived" within the framework of the Black Church.

The conversations and the memories of the first U.S. King, Oba Oseijeman of Oyotunji Village, are priceless. I remember well the teachings of many of the elders that Dr. Eason cites from the years I spent with the people of Oyotunji. In the *Itanle*, the historical narrative of my community, we have submitted to collective memory a line that states, "Dancer who became King." He was the first African-American to be initiated into an African-based spirituality. His history must be retained for he was a great visionary and leader. He was born to be King; he never abandoned his vision and always sought to keep it free of practices and ideologies that were not *authentically* from ancient Africa. The life of the Oba and his ability to materialize the ancestral memories of Yorubaland and what was once Dahomey validates the ability of African descendants to receive support, inspiration, and information from our originating ancestors.

Another important feature of this chapter is the information Dr. Eason shares with the reader about the ancestral masquerade and the importance of its concealed powers. Egungun is the physical appearance of a deified ancestor of an entire family, clan, or group. It embodies the combination of genetic factors and noble personality traits that have secured the descendant's existence today. The design of the masquerade characterizes a collective spiritual reality as opposed to an individual physical reality.

In other words, as Dr. Eason points out, veneration of our ancestors constitutes a calibrated philosophical and ethical search for collective wisdom, knowledge and understanding. The appearance of Egungun makes us aware that there is more going on than meets the eye. Egungun demonstrates the ability of its descendants to take something that appears to be immobile and make it get up and dance. Egungun exemplifies the uninterrupted connection between the past, present, and future.

Once again the author leads us to Ile-Ife in Chapter Four. In this section he cites ancient facets of the annual Ifa Festival and explains its more recent adaptations.

He shares with the reader many of the rituals that are not readily visible to the many international visitors that attend the festival each year. The translations of the songs sung during the Ifa Festival will benefit efforts in the Diasporic communities that will establish their own Ifa celebrations. He describes the ritual care of the Ooni of Ife's, Yoruba King-of-Kings, sacred *ikin* and the ritual of washing Ifa. Although many Ifa adherents think that the festival is conducted in the same manner that it was historically, Dr. Eason documents the various changes that were made to accommodate contemporary lifestyles.

Once again, the author questions the mythical role of women such as the Arugba in the creation stories,

First Commentary: Accepting Destiny

and the contemporary refusal to allow women full participation in Ifa rituals. Women often appear to be a full partner but this partnership does not extend to Ifa priesthood, economics, or the distribution of work in Ifa. Gender parity in the Yoruba Diaspora has not yet been reached.

Dr. Eason's sensitivity and awareness concerning the inequities of gender roles is refreshing. These issues have not been acknowledged or addressed by either scholars or practitioners from the perspective presented in this work. It is my hope that this book encourages more investigative writings on the role of women in Ifa. What women bring to the table of spiritual and cultural evolution is being wasted or minimized, because of bias and gender prejudices, not because of sacred doctrine.

In the first part of Chapter five Dr. Eason depicts Oyotunji Village's Ifa Festival as a time of reunion and celebration. The author writes in depth about rituals in Gary that were similar to those in Ile-Ife and those that were different than those he had experienced in Nigeria. One of the first points of departure was the dancing of the King's 'Odu' and the Esu/Elegba dance performed by men and women. It was the females that demonstrated the sexual themes associated with Esu/Elegba's constant arousal.

The second section, and perhaps the most controversial, is Dr. Eason's description of his first initiation to Ifa in Gary. He describes it as not having any of the accoutrements of other Yoruba-based initiations to Ifa. This brings out the question of the importance of ritualism and physical implements.

Is it the ritual that gives *ase* or sacred power to the initiate, or does it come directly from the divinities? He notes that his initiation in Gary was improvised and indigenous, implying that it lacked the *"official"* procedures of Ile-Ife so an Ifa initiation in Oyotunji followed. Therefore, when Dr. Eason had a consultation performed for him in Ile-Ife the rite performed in the Village was accepted by Ifa in Ile-Ife. This seems to imply that the deities are not as limited by the mechanics and materials of ceremonies as humans can be. Ingredients and procedures are things that set limits on humanity's relationship to spirit. Fortunately, spirit is not bound by these limitations. In many areas of the Yoruba Diaspora access to the power of the divinities focuses on the status of the humans performing the ceremonies as opposed to an understanding that *ase* is bestowed upon us by the Source of all things.

According to Dr. Eason a difference between Ile-Ife and Oyotunji Festivals was the appearance of Egungun. The appearance of Egungun seems to always be appropriate in the "New Yoruba Movement" during an important ritual or occasion because of the role of the collective wisdom contained by and made available by the ancestors. It is through ancestral assistance and determination concerning the continuity of African spirituality that those descendants in the United States have been able to recapture their spirituality and culture.

In the Afterword Dr. Eason's main ideas are continuity and change. The development of Oyotunji and the New Yoruba Movement that started in the late 1950s still continues. The ideas of "The Medahochi" that Dr. Eason quotes contains nuggets of encouragement around accepting the fact that we are indigenous Yoruba living in the West; this is a seed that I predict will grow. After reading this manuscript I can only express the pride I feel and accept the prompting that says I must continue. The path

First Commentary: Accepting Destiny

we have chosen is difficult, full of controversy, challenges, and at times ridicule.

The intention that has kept me steadfast on this path for thirty years is captured in a portion of sacred text called *Obara Irete*. One of the energies that *Obara Irete* identifies is the cessation and beginning of time and it emphasizes the unifying element of the moment. Using time as a matrix helps me sort out the *infinities* that are always present in the sacred texts of Ifa's layered messages. To paraphrase the proverb, *Obara Irete*, it tells us that *yesterday* stops its forward movement in order to greet *tomorrow*. When *yesterday* stops, it is not uncommon for today to be a time of sadness—His Royal Highness Oba Efuntola Oseijeman Adelabu Adefunmi I, "The Medahochi", Iya Kpojito Hwesihuno, Chief Elemosha Awolowo, and Chief Dr Djisovi Eason Iba se! In other words, the times of the past are an important feature of the present, otherwise how will we build a better future?

Consider this book as a symbolic seed and then think of how a seed says goodbye: to the comfort and warmth of the earth, to that which is familiar; to the safety of emulating what you see others do. It is easy to remain a child and difficult to begin to make arrangement for what best suits your family constructs, yet a beautiful blossom is the valedictorian of the seed, and a piece of fruit is the seed's hope for tomorrow. Imitating this natural form of time confrontation is the only way we can be sure that we have done the internal work that will allow us in the Diaspora to move into our tomorrow. It is important that through his writing, Dr. Eason allows us to spend some time looking yesterday in the face so we can move into tomorrow.

E'ku ise Baba!!!

Second Commentary
Eason on Ifa

Akinloye Ojo

The late Dr. Louis Djisovi Ikukomi Eason provides an historical and solicitous study of some aspects of the religious practices and festivals that are included in the veneration of the Yorùbá divination deity, Ifá Òrúnmìlà, in West Africa and North America. Ilé Ifè, the Yorùbá primordial home town in Nigeria, West Africa and Òyótúnjí, the North American Yorùbá settlement in South Carolina, North America are the two focused centers of Yorùbá religious practices on the continent and in the Diaspora. The practices and festivals within the compared locales allow Dr Eason to identify ancient elements of Ifá worship and practices primarily in Ilé Ifè and their contemporary materializations in both circumstances. He moves away from the popular but limited notion in the Diaspora that Ifá is simply a system of divination, and he asserts that Ifá is both a Yorùbá deity (whose physical manifestation is Òrúnmìlà and therefore the same deity) and a Yorùbá system of beliefs and sacred rituals and traditions. This assertion is made very early in the first chapter of the book. The intentionality of the claim and its location in the first lines is to serve the ethnographic and autobiographic purposes of the author.

This book is written to provide information on Ifá religious traditions of Yorùbá people in Nigeria and the Diaspora. It is also written to specifically highlight the continuity of these traditions amongst the new Yorùbá of Òyótúnjí as they reclaim the ancient traditions that slavery and racial prejudice have abducted from them. It is consequentially written to give an insider account of the (religious) life in the African Diaspora. This is an account that shows how members of this Diaspora (highlighted by Dr Eason), struggling with racial injustice and violence, staggered from one religious encounter to another before drawing on Ifá religious traditions to proclaim and sustain an African religious identity. The majority of its content is therefore drawn from the personal life stories of the key participants, particularly that of Dr. Eason himself. The extraction begins from his earliest religious, political and spiritual experiences all the way to his later observations and participation, for over three decades, in Ifá religious practices. There is the hope that the contents will provide knowledge and information to younger (as well as unaware) members of the communities in Nigeria and the Diaspora. In scrutinizing both the structural and functional elements of religion and religious practices in the lives of Yorùbá people in West Africa and North America, this book is able to organize and present information about Ifá religious practices and the momentous roles that Ifa plays in the identity and survival of the Yorùbá people worldwide particularly as the source of knowledge on all natural and supernatural aspects of their daily existence.

Second Commentary: Eason on Ifa

This book is divided into six parts consisting of five chapters and a short summary of its contents presented as the afterword. The chapters are loosely linked primarily by cross-referencing done by the author and appear to have been independently written. Each provides the author's exhaustive treatment of the focused issue such as the centrality of Ilé Ifè to Ifá religious tradition. Notwithstanding, they are progressively organized with each contributing to the pioneering goals of the author. In spite of its organization and uniqueness, the perspective of analyzing structural and functional elements of the religious history and behavior of Ifá devotees in both Ilé Ifè and Òyótúnjí (and to a limited extent, their clients) from which the book is written and the adoption of the autobiographical trope by the author, particularly through the emblematic use of personal narratives for rhetorical effect, combine to seemingly transform the book into a rather telescopic study. He thus departs from other approaches at understanding the constitution of Ifá.[1]

As the primal source of all knowledge and wisdom within Yorùbá society, Ifá (Orunmila) is renowned amongst its devotees and the larger Yorùbá society as a circumlocutory oracle whose vocalizations to those who consult it for advice are seldom simple or direct. Ifá's responses to enquiries are mostly presented in the form of Odù Ifá (marks or standards through which Ifá's wisdom governs all situations in the world and readable only to the diviner) and its accompanying verses known as Esè Ifá (collection of proverbs, poems, songs, stories, and myths about Yorùbá life upon which issues raised by the Odu will be resolved).[2] Therefore, a diviner seeking to help his client through Ifá divination can only understand the remedy from the principal deity through the emerged

Odu and the subtext contained in the appropriate Èsè Ifá.[3] Likewise, the narrative as well as the analytical focus of each chapter in the book must be understood in order to better understand the work.

It is indeed an ethnographic study, in its focus on Ifá religious practices but with a significant studious incorporation of the autobiographies of a principal character (the King of Òyótúnjí) and the ethnographer, who non fortuitously, is a devotee-convert. The book must, therefore, be perceived as a self-story whose critical goal is the preservation of the religious traditions of "indigenous Africans" inescapably linked, due to the transatlantic slave trade, to the "New Africans" in the Diaspora be they the Diaspora devotees in Cuba or Brazil or the New Yorùbá in Òyótúnjí. However, unlike any other self-stories used as mediums for the preservation of indigenous religious traditions,[4] the preserved traditions in this book are in reality withering and fading amongst the indigenous people while intensifying amongst the Diaspora people in the Americas. The strengthening of these traditions have thus inspired the New Yorùbá to re-affirm their African religious identity and work hard at salvaging specific aspects of African religious traditions lost during and after the end of the inhumane institution of slavery in the Americas. It can only be hoped that the intensification of these religious practices amongst the New Yorùbá will spur a significant revival amongst the traditional, indigenous Yorùbá people on the continent.

CHAPTER ONE

The first chapter on the "historiocity of Africa Religious Tradition and Festivals in North America" serves as the introduction to the book. It in effect introduces the subject matter, the contents of the book, and the author, especially the centrality of his personal story to the socio-religious comparative study done in the work. In the chapter, the author provides a pithy but generalized introduction to Ifá and the transcendent and communal religion that is associated with it. Ifá religion is presented as a communal system of faith that signifies the sacred Yorùbá worldview, as contained in "beliefs, ritualistic practices, moral and ethical standards that have been traditionally transmitted from one generation of Yorùbá to successive others." Devoting the early part of the chapter to the description of Ifá as the epitome of Yorùbá spirituality and religious traditions, the author reckoned that the salient feature of these religious traditions among the Yorùbá is the emphatic maintenance of a balance between the cosmic sphere and the human life force.

Finally, in this condensed introduction to Ifá religion, the author states that these all encompassing traditions are persevering, particularly amongst the Yorùbá today, in redacted forms having survived the trans-Atlantic slave trade (a 16th to 19th century holocaust according to the author), the incursions of Islam and Christianity, European colonialism and racial discrimination.

Essentially, to it its devotees in West Africa and in the Diaspora, Ifá religious practices harmonize their earthly concerns and difficulties with Ifá's (and other Deities') prepotency in solving human problems. Ifá disentangles the physical problems of the devotees as well as those tribulations that can only be unraveled at a higher celestial plane.

As engaging as we find it, there are two practical concerns with Dr Eason's brief introduction of Ifá religion. The first is the comparison of Ifá divination to catholic confessional. While this is clearly an attempt to provide some form of understanding for the uninitiated reader, it may detract from the essence of Ifá divination. Ifá divination is more than purging the soul for the believer. As it has been noted in numerous works on Ifá divination,[5] the priest and the devotee or client are trying to access knowledge of the past in order to identify the source of particular problems and simultaneously ascertain the solution through Ifá's predictions.

Secondly, Dr. Eason in his analysis and reliance on indigenous sources appears to decry the dominance of the Western, Eurocentric lexis in the discussions about Africa and Afrocentric issues. Unfortunately, the author appears to be engaging the same tools as he attempts to date the appearance of Ifá in this chapter. He provides a sufferable submission that this occurred thousands of years ago but the knowledge of Yorùbá mythology and Ifá narratives inform us Ifá Orunmila was with the Supreme Being at creation. Dr. Eason would later provide a detailed discussion of this point in later chapters but it appears that there was a succumbing to the practice in ethnographic studies of providing date or period of origin.

The latter part of the chapter provides an autobiographical narrative on the author and his conversion to the Ifá religion. This is more than just an introduction to the life of the author. It serves a multitude of not too perceptible purposes. First, it provides an accessible illustration of the soulfulness of the contents of the study. The book is written on the accounts of Dr. Eason's life from his sheltered but knowledge driven childhood, through his youth that was dominated by activism and fight for racial justice and onto his adulthood that was pervaded by his experiences as a participant-observer of Ifá religion. The life story in the introductory chapter must also be seen as an emphasis of the author's lamentation on the lack of published comparative cross cultural studies of Ifá. The inclusion of this personal narrative in the introductory chapter also highlights the mixed methods engaged in the study. The story of the author's life provides both an ethnographic as well as literary narrative but more importantly, it is the distillation of the contents of the book. In Dr. Eason's life story (as well as the book), one encounters a new devotee to Ifá religion, who is seeking to identify with his new found religion, not at his point of conversion within his vicinity but at the essential core of the faith. This unavoidably presents a cross-cultural comparison of the new faith, Ifá religion through the life of this educated, social activist of a convert.

CHAPTER TWO

In chapter two, Dr. Eason localizes the origin of both the Ifá religious practices and the Yorùbá people in Ilé Ifè and then proceeds to outline the contents of Ifá. The focus of the first part of the chapter is on the history of the Yorùbá legendary city of Ilé Ifè and its importance to the study of Ifá religious practices and festivals. The story of Ilé Ifè, the hub of Ifá-lore and the ancestral home of the Yorùbá people, has been made extraordinary by the many mythological and historical accounts. It has therefore become an awesome location for both indigenous Africans and others, such as the author, whose socio-religious encounters have brought them to the city. This is notwithstanding aspects of the oral traditions of various Yorùbá communities that indicate that there were multiple locales known as Ilé Ifè prior to the current location. It is this that has driven the contention amongst historians that the current Ilé Ifè is not the subject of the numerous myths and historical narratives, a point reiterated by the author. In fact, he rightfully asserts that even though Ifá religious practices pervade Yorùbá land and beyond, any study of Ifá must include the ancient city. The centrality of Ilé Ifè to the religious practices derives from Ifá Òrúnmìlà, the divination deity, landing there from heaven with his system of knowledge. In highlighting the critical position of Ilé Ifè to Ifá religion, the book ventures into the origins of Yorùbá religion and culture.

Dr. Eason states that questions surrounding the origins of Yorùbá religion and culture are not settled and unfortunately, these are not in any way resolved in the book either. Significantly, this is not the purpose of either the book or the chapter. Overall, he provides an evenhanded discussion on Yorùbá civilization drawing, interestingly, from both Yorùbá oral and written traditions. The most luminous aspect of the discussion is the effortlessness in which the deductions and suppositions of the verbal and published sources are integrated to outline the contents of the varied versions of Yorùbá history. Even then, it is interesting that with the availability of sources (it is impossible not to notice the comprehensive listing of remarkable sources in the footnotes) on Yorùbá history and culture, he presents important summations rather than an in-depth discussion of the people's history. This is not the purpose of the book and considering the focus, the discussions presented appear adequate.

In the second part of the chapter, he turns his attention to a more detailed description of Ifá: its description amongst traditional Yorùbá people; its priesthood including the sixteen priests of Oòni, the Yorùbá principal monarch of Ilé Ifè; and the "female principles" found in Ifá. Additionally, the chapter provides the author's theoretical consideration of two issues. First is the essence of Ifá as an applied Afrocentric religious science and second is the analysis of Ifá as the deity that truly "knows it all." This part of the chapter contains some of the more weighty considerations of Ifá Òrúnmìlà both as a significant Yorùbá deity as well as representing a meaningful and advantageous system of divination and knowledge sharing. The rise of the Ifá system is given as being enshrouded in a Yorùbá worldview, driven by the metaphysical principle concept of àse (divine energy). Àse being the "energy, power or force" through which things are done. The chapter goes on to elucidate the relationship between àse, the ancestors and the Supreme Being – the ultimate source of àse.

Much as one is in agreement with him regarding the importance of àse, it is difficult not to remark that the idea of the concept's centrality to Ifá religion is more renowned amongst Ifá practitioners and scholars in the Diaspora. In spite of the work done by people such as Rowland Abiodun on àse and Yorùbá creativity, it would be interesting to know the opinions of most Ifá practitioners in Nigeria on this issue and the relationship of the concept to the more practical power of "àwíse" (speaking things into being). Dr. Eason focuses mostly on data collected in Benin in this section of the book. In presenting Ifá as an applied Afrocentric religious science, he lays out the Ifá divination process and illustrates some of the modalities that the diviner follows in using the Odù and the appropriate Esè Ifá to address the concerns of the client or other devotees. The discussion also touches on the variety of myths in various Yorùbá descendant or related communities in West Africa.

Appropriately, the chapter then addresses the palpable question of why Ifá Òrúnmìlà is all knowing and capable of solving a multitude of problems. The consensus belief amongst all practitioners in West Africa and beyond (no matter how they perceive the name, being or story of Ifá Òrúnmìlà) is that Ifá is the "Eléri Ìpín", meaning the witness at creation. This is the basis for his pristine *theory of Eleri Ipin*. Having been a witness at creation, Ifá knows the nature of the Universe and since he was there when the destiny of all things was being determined, Ifá is able to know the past, mediate with the present and predict the future. In essence, as the deity that knew everything from the beginning of the earth, Ifá Òrúnmìlà is therefore instinctively the "all knowing" amongst current residents of the earth. As he fittingly discusses, Ifá's status as the Eléri Ìpín is the conjectural basis for Ifá's role in the Yorùbá belief in predestination.

The book does not address this but this is the major reason why the Yorùbá people go through the process, *"Wíwo Esèntaye"* (or probing a child's destiny) for every new born. The family of the new born child will consult Ifá through the diviner to probe the destiny of the new arrival and receive instructions on things such as safeguarding the destiny, pacifying spirits or deities that might affect the destiny and all other necessary rituals and activities needed to ensure growth and development of the child. Minus the religious emphasis, this is analogous to the post natal visit to the pediatrician at which a child's medical dos and don'ts are identified and listed for the parents.

The chapter ends with a laconic consideration of Ifá priesthood. It considers the training modalities and rigor involved. It also provides a description of the tools used by various Ifá priests and the variations that the author has noted in their tools and mode of divination. These observations were drawn from fieldwork done by Dr. Eason from as early at 1979 in Òyótúnjí and later periods in Nigeria and Benin. The discussion of the priesthood narrows its focus on the sixteen Ifá priests known as Awoni. These priests serve the Oòni and are quite important in Ifá festival and religious ceremonies. Interestingly, the chapter ends with the feminist theory driven discussion of the role and importance of women in Ifá religion, particularly, the priesthood. He gives a pithy mythological and historical account of the central role of women in Ifá religion and Yorùbá life. Citing Odù Òsà Méjì to highlight the provided reasons for women's loss of political and civil authority, the author argues, as other feminist and anti-hegemonic scholars have before, that significant male trickery and outsiders' manipulations have taken place to change the status of women in Ifá religion and the larger society. Despite its strength, including the etymological analysis of the Yorùbá word, Babalawo, the consideration of this issue appears to be driven by the controversy about whether women can be Ifá priests (awo ifá). This is a contentious issue, especially in the Diaspora and amongst modern Ifá practitioners, and which the author would like to see resolved to return women to their esteemed status in Ifá religion.

CHAPTER THREE

The third chapter contains the detailed history of the Òyótúnjí movement from 1959 when Nana Oseijeman was initiated into the Yorùbá priesthood of Obatala. Previously known as Walter King until 1957 when he changed his name, Oseijeman would eventually succeed in his personal quest for his African cultural and socio-religious root. This was a personal attainment that will transform into a communal achievement in Òyótúnjí. The history is presented first to add to the meager number of available historical accounts on the movement. Essentially, Dr. Eason anticipates the chapter, as well as the book, to fill the inherent void in the study of such movements as Òyótúnjí that were for the revitalization of African religious and socio-cultural practices amongst African Americans. The chapter is also presented as a background for the comparative discussions that are done in later chapters on the Ifá religious practices found in Ilé Ifè and in Òyótúnjí. The most significant knowledge from the history of the movement and the creation of the unique New Yorùbá settlement of Òyótúnjí African Village in Sheldon, South Carolina is the fact that African Americans were able to discover, reclaim and revitalize African religious practices that several years of slavery and racial injustice has nearly exterminated amongst the African American community or for that matter in the entire African Diaspora. This is more momentous when one considers that the very beginnings of the Òyótúnjí (Ifá) religious movement was in the era of the 1950s when most African Americans were eagerly aspiring for change in the racial politics of the country and assiduously seeking the benefits of social and economic integration as opposed to any affinity towards Africa. But the members of the New Yorùbá movement found resurrection in repossessing their African identity – as the name of the physical settlement occupied by the movement indicates:

i.

Òyó   tún   jí   = Òyótúnjí.
(trad/ Yorùbá) (again) (to wake up) = Oyo have woken again

Second Commentary: Eason on Ifa

Dr. Eason provides an extraordinary active history of the movement by providing biographical information on the founder and leader of the Òyótúnjí movement. As with the autobiographical details about Dr. Eason provided in chapter one, we become familiar with the personal struggles and the socio-religious encounters that gave birth to the movement in New York. The story of Oba Oseijeman therefore becomes the story of the New Yorùbá movement. The expansion of the leadership circle within the group and relocation of the group to a permanent area in the South is thus a testimony to the rebirth and conversion of Oseijeman and his tight knit group to the new but old Yorùbá worldview. It becomes obvious in the chapter that the growth of the movement is predicated by the development in the personal narratives of the leaders of the group who continue to grow in knowledge and practice of the Yorùbá traditional religion. The ultimate source of knowledge and validation for this group and by extension, the movement was Ilé Ifè. Nonetheless notable influence also comes from the group's knowledge of and relationship with Afro-Cubans and other African descendants in the Diaspora. For the New Yorùbá people, the Ifá religion inspires the reconnection with their ancestral past and challenges their intellectual capabilities to decipher the elements of their own African identity long castigated by the larger, western culture dominated American society.

CHAPTER FOUR

Chapter four of the book represents the best opportunity for the reader to get a better appreciation of the ethnographic work done by the author. It is the chapter in which the combination of the literary and ethnographic modes in the book has yielded the best outcome in terms of narrative clarity and idea development. The chapter provides a description of the annual Ifá/New Year festival in Ilé Ifè (as witnessed by the author in 1992 during his fieldwork at the then University of Ife). Situated within the narrative is an analysis of the importance of the festival to the Ifá religion as well as the lives of the Yorùbá Ifá traditionalists. The contents and significance of each aspect of the festival in past celebrations is discussed as well as the changes in the contemporary commemoration. Traditionally celebrated at the end of June, the festival is now held during the first weekend of the month. There have also been changes in the length of time for each stage of the festival with the number of days reduced. In spite of all the current modifications, the annual festival provides all Ifá devotees an opportunity for communal worship. The devotees join forces to celebrate the importance of the religion to their individual and collective lives.

The chapter describes the activities of each day of the extended festival as it concerns the different groups of participants. In addition, the traditional versus contemporary transformations of the events, people and places are continually noted with the description of festival period. These descriptive narratives are then complemented with more Ifá Òrúnmìlà related myths and stories signifying, once again, Ifá's indispensable value to the survival and wellbeing of the devotees. In the consideration of the roles of the different important participants of the extended festival, Dr. Eason alludes again to the limited role of women (especially female Ifá priests) in the festival and by extension in the public display of Ifá religion. Other elements of the festivals such as the Ifá songs and prayers and blessings shared are discussed. A significant number of illustrations of these songs and prayers along with the discussion of their contents and sanctifying values are also provided.

Based on the detailed narratives and the incisive analysis, it becomes apparent that Dr. Eason was both an analytic researcher and an enthralled and involved participant (along with his wife) at the annual festival. More than any other part of the chapter, the last section in which he provides a personal reflection on participating in the annual festival and his comparison of the religious experience with other life changing religious encounters (involving himself and others such as Malcolm X and Chief Adeniji Raji, the author's host in Lagos) provides a clear illustration of the dual role of the author. Beyond the research work, he as a practitioner and Ifá priest gets a new Ifá name signifying victory over death; receives audience with the Oòni of Ifè; interacts with the Awoni chiefs of Ilé Ifè and even gets to participate with the worldwide representation of diviners in unity rituals at the annual festival. The concluding comments at the end of the chapter best state the socio-religious importance of the Ifá festival in the life of the author and other Ifá devotees in the Diaspora, especially those that are part of the Òyótúnjí settlement in North America.

CHAPTER FIVE

In line with its comparative purpose, the fifth chapter of the book is devoted to discussions about the replicate Ifá festival amongst the New Yorùbá people in Òyótúnjí. Interestingly, the festival, again witnessed by the author, was in 1992 which was a milestone in the history of the New Yorùbá people of Òyótúnjí. The reported festival marked the twentieth anniversary of the Ifá festival amongst these new world devotees. The chapter and the discussion therein benefit tremendously from the laudable ethnographic narrative provided in chapter four. However, one would have liked the narrative about the various festival activities in Òyótúnjí to be more constricted and may be followed by a socio-religious and comparative analysis of both festivals. It becomes obvious from the account in this chapter that the revelries in Ilé Ifè were etched in the mind of the author and they appear to have been value marked as the inventive practices. It must be noted that another possible reason for this could the fact that the 1992 Ifá festival was the first witnessed by the author, even though he had been an initiated Ifá priest since 1979. It therefore becomes more understandable why the events of Òyótúnjí were unavoidably viewed with a far more critical, proportional, but considerate lenses and basically marked as reinventions. This is not a highly critical issue as the history of Òyótúnjí and the New Yorùbá people and that of Ifá religion provided the basis for this approach. Indeed, the author had reiterated the point in the previous chapters that Ilé Ifè was the origin of Ifá religion and that the modern practices in Nigeria, Òyótúnjí and elsewhere were redactions of traditional practices in Ilé Ifè.

Appropriately themed as "a time of destiny," the 1992 Òyótúnjí Ifá festival allows the New Yorùbá in Òyótúnjí to venerate Ifá Òrúnmìlà and indirectly celebrate the Supreme Being who, by creating Ifá, allowing him to witness all creation, and endowing him with the knowledge and power to decipher all human problems, has essentially attributed all power to Himself. As the author rightly notes, "Olódùmarè is (therefore) indirectly worshipped as "the first and final causes" of everything that happens when Ifá is consulted for causes of and resolutions to problems and worshipped for bringing harmony out of chaotic situations." This schema of a deity –such as Ifá Òrúnmìlà– owing his existence to Olódùmarè, the Supreme Being and source of all things is the cornerstone of the Yorùbá religious life. Expressively, this played a significant role in the conversion of the mostly Christian African Americans that were to reclaim the traditional Ifá religion as theirs in Òyótúnjí. This was covertly presented in chapter three but the effect of this conversion here is apparent in some of the modifications and omissions in the rituals of the Ifá festival at Òyótúnjí. More so, unlike in Ilé Ifè where Yorùbá culture is apparently exalted in a location that is geographically central to Yorùbá society, Ifá devotees in Òyótúnjí have to be mindful of the western and Christian milieu in which they find themselves. There is also that constant concern or for lack of a better word, agony amongst the Ifá priests in Òyótúnjí about whether the priests and devotees in Ilé Ifè will doubt the validity of their rituals and practices in the Diaspora.

Dr Eason provides a detailed description of the annual religious celebration that is held in conjunction with the annual "New Yorùbá" National Convention. The narrative of the festival presented includes all the preliminary activities such as the colorful parade and dance that occurs in the courtyard of Òyótúnjí's King, Oba Oseijeman and the consultations done in the temple of Obatala, the patron divinity of Òyótúnjí. The Ifá Egungun ritual was the next event in the festival. The ritual involving the symbolic return of Yorùbá and Òyótúnjí ancestors gives the Oba and the priests the chance to advocate collective recollection of ancestral powers and their significance and benefits to the community. The following event in the festival included a ceremony of allegiance to Ilé Ifè and Òyótúnjí Village that is held in the Ogboni-

Shango Temples of the king's compound. The top echelon of the leadership of the Òyótúnjí movement in North America participates in this event. It is here that the king and leader for the movement, Oba Oseijeman gives his speech on the significance of the settlement, the culture and the religion to the New Yorùbá community in the Diaspora. The allegiance ceremony is then followed by the Odù reciting ritual that directly involves the male Ifá priests and indirectly, their wives and the female priests. This reciting and performance ritual ends the sacramental aspect of the festival. Unique to Òyótúnjí, the festival is said to be transformed into an annul New Yorùbá (academic) conference. The gathering, in 1992, primarily involved itself in the consideration of gender and Ifá priesthood and secondarily, the indigenization of the Ifá system in North America. It is interesting that the primary issue at the focused conference was gender and Ifá priesthood. This is an issue of concern for the author throughout the book and it is revitalizing to see that the religious experiences that he and his wife had in Ilé Ifè played a major role in the deliberations on gender and Ifá priesthood during the festival in Òyótúnjí. It becomes apparent that the proposed indigenization of the Ifá system as well as the reformation of the role of women in Ifá religion were driven by practical needs but greatly hindered by the concern for validation and affirmation from Ilé Ifè.

In conclusion, Dr Eason has drawn from reasonable written and oral sources to provide a socio-historical comparative analysis of Ifá religion via its festivals in Nigeria and North America. He has provided focal insights into the transportation of these festivals into the Diaspora, particularly North America as well as the further transformations of these religious festivals in West Africa and North America. He provides insights that are not limited to the festivals but covers the practitioners in both places as well. In between the transporting and transforming, the book also highlights the fortitude of Ifá religion and its devotees as they cope with the impacts of colonialism, slavery, racism, socio-political upheavals and renewable onslaught of other religions over the years. As noted by the author in the early chapters, the purpose and contents of the book make it the first of its kind. We are not aware of any other work that has done a comprehensive 'cross-comparative' religious study on Ifá festivals in Ilé Ifè, Nigeria and Òyótúnjí in Sheldon, North Carolina as this book. It is definitely a significant contribution to the better understanding of both ancient and contemporary religious practices of Ifá Òrúnmìlà and his devotees in Nigeria and the Diaspora. The memoir of this participant observer is significant because of perspective that he brings from his strategic positioning. All of the principals and most of the founding members have died without formally publishing their memoirs. Dr. Eason was present when Oba was called Baba and operated as priest of a cultural center in Sheldon, South Carolina. Subsequent to the center's relocation to the present site, it was renamed Oyotunji African Village, and the villagers coronated Oseijeman. Throughout this period, Dr. Eason was a first-hand observer and was on conversational, as well priestly terms, with the Oba and his first initiates and their wives, and he knew other early initiates and associates.

References

Abimbola, Wande. 1968. *Ijinle Ohun Enu Ifa*. Glasgow: Collins

_____. 2005. *Awon Oju Odu Mereerindinlogun*. Ibadan: University Press Plc.

Bascom, William. 1993. *Sixteen Cowries: Yoruba Divination from Africa to the New World*. First Midland Book Edition. Bloomington: Indiana University Press

Epega, Afolabi & Philip Neimark. 1995. *The Sacred Ifa Oracle*. San Francisco: Harper Collins Publishers

Notes

1. Dr. Eason, drawing from Abimbola (1975) and others, provides a description of what Ifa is in Chapter 2.
2. Wande Abimbola, *Ijinle Ohun Enu Ifa* (Glasgow: Collins, 1968), 16
3. Wande Abimbola, *Awon Oju Odu Mereerindinlogun* (Ibadan: University Press Plc, 2005), xi - xxviii
4. See the works of Malidoma Patrice Some and his life as a member of the Dagara people in West Africa: Malidoma, Some (1993; 19951997; 1999) or visit http://www.schoolofwisdom.com/Malidoma/elder.html
5. See bibliographies provided in the works of Bascom (1961, 1969 and 1980).

Acknowledgements

In completing this work, I stand on the shoulders of several keepers of Ifa traditions and rituals in Nigeria and in the United States. I would like to express my special gratitude to two who died in early 2005: Oba Oseijeman (King of the Oyotunji African Village, Sheldon, South Carolina) and Chief Mayegun 'Bayo Ogundijo (a Yoruba cultural specialist at Obafemi Awolowo University, Ile-Ife); respectively, they introduced me to Ifa divination and provided me with opportunities to connect with cultural informers and resources. Professors Wande Abimbola (Awise —an Ifa priestly title honoring his contributions to Ifa scholarship) and 'Bade Ajuwon (specialist in African cultural studies and literatures) were among the initial supporters of my field studies in Ile-Ife; both were familiar with the local communities and were affiliated with the Obafemi Awolowo University library, which had a substantial collection of books and manuscripts. I extend my profound thanks to Medahochi Kofi Omowale Zanu (my godfather and a founding member of the Oyotunji African Village Movement) for sharing his passion for learning and knowledge of Ifa with me for nearly three decades.

I fondly remember the late Babatunde Olatunji (famed percussionist from Nigeria) for introducing me to the spirituality and diverse genres of African cultural arts performance. Much of what I learned while attending his Center in Harlem during the 1970s is reflected in aspects of this work. Bishop Alfred Norris (United Methodist Church and the Interdenominational Theological Center, Atlanta) facilitated my studies and research in African theology and music by funding my first travel to Nigeria.

I am grateful for the conferences that gave me opportunities to present my research and interpretations and receive helpful comments for this manuscript. In this regard, I refer in particular to conferences convened by Professors Toyin Falola (University of Texas-Austin) and Jacob Olupona (Harvard University). They encouraged me in my work and provided opportunities for me to refine my thinking.

My deepest appreciation is extended to Professors William E. Grant (retired, Bowling Green State University-Ohio) and Rowland Abiodun (Amherst College) for providing intellectual insight and mentoring that encouraged me to complete this manuscript. Professor Abiodun's specialized knowledge of Ifa and other Yoruba traditions was immensely helpful to me as I sought to identify sources for research and analyze cultural documents.

I will forever be grateful to my wife (who already held the Ph.D. in history when we met in January 1984) for her unwavering love and for her contributions to my development as a scholar. From my sophomore year as a non-traditional student through my receipt of the Ph.D., she was an ardent supporter as well as a research associate. This manuscript could not have been completed without her intellectual input that is infused throughout the manuscript.

Finally, I profoundly appreciate those beautiful people who contributed indirectly to this book—my birth sons (Kojo, Kwaku, and Amansu Eason), my grandson ("Bumi" Darik Schaaf), and my godsons Babacar M'Baye, Glenn Johnson, Seneca Vaught, Zachery Williams) and goddaughters (Camillia Z. Rodgers and Luwanda Scott-Vaught). My love and high regard for them motivated me to strive to complete this manuscript as part of my legacy. Peace and love!

PART B

THE TEXT

Chapter 1

Memories and Observations on Ifa Religion and Culture in Ile-Ife and Oyotunji

My memoir combines vicarious knowledge gleaned from scientific studies with first-hand observations from my sojourn in Yoruba Traditional Religion as a participant over thirty-odd years. In 1971 I helped to relocate the Oyotunji African Village on its present site in Sheldon, South Carolina—just outside of Beaufort on Highway 21. Within a short while, Chief Elemosha assigned me to various roles in the cultural activities in the Village. Oyotunji may be translated as the revival or return of the Yorubas, meaning African Americans who revivified Yoruba religion and lifestyles in the United States. Throughout this manuscript, I use New Yoruba, Oyotunji Yoruba, African-American Yoruba, and Black American Yoruba interchangeably when referring to residents of and loyalists living outside Oyotunji Village. My long association inclines me to say that I stand on the shoulders of my Oyotunji elders who taught me much of what I now share in this memoir.

Prior to its present relocation, I frequented the Village but became more intimate with it subsequent to the move. I was privy to conversations about how the Oba and his cohorts were trying to build a replica of a traditional Yoruba town, meaning that it would be rustic, not modern in architecture, plumbing and electrical infrastructure.[1] Their ideas about what the village should be derived primarily from early twentieth-century publications that inferred a virtually static Yoruba religion and mythic culture, frozen in a nebulous traditional time warp. The thought that African Americans who were revivifying Yoruba Traditional culture inside the United States could not avoid innovation continuously needled them. They had to keep a wary eye on state health and building-code inspectors, who might try to force them to abandon or modernize essential aspects of their plans. In the 1970s, the Oyotunji Yorubas did all that they could to avoid being represented as innovators. They retold myths from Ifa orature and tried to be exacting in duplicating what they read and observed of religious rituals and practices. For years their approach colored my thought about, and attraction to, African traditions.

Traditions and prototypic characters from the primal past have palpable presence in the lives of contemporary *orisha* worshippers, conveying the impression that they believe the religion is unchanging. This is not unlike the average Christian who gives little thought to historical changes and the processes of redacting Scriptures and shifting lifestyles that brought the religion to the point that they know today. In other words, acknowledged or not, there have been transformations throughout the history of these religions. The traditional, New Year event—the annual Ifa Festivals in Ile-Ife, Nigeria and the Oyotunji African Village in Sheldon, South Carolina—reflects significant transformative features in the Yoruba Traditional Religion. Reflection on this change and how acknowledgement of it can be used to revivify aspects of Yoruba Traditionalism is the primary theme that I address in this book.

The Ifa Festival that I attended in Ile-Ife in 1992 was my first. I was captivated. It was commemorative, educational, festive, performance-oriented, and otherworldly in its rituals that celebrated the *orisha* (Yoruba deity, divinity, god/ess) of knowledge and wisdom, Ifa. It was a celebration presided over and performed by the *Awon*i (priestly counselors to the *Ooni*—traditional king of Ile-Ife) and other members of the Ifa priesthood selected to assist. Private rituals preceded the public spectacle.[2] Because of the participatory dynamic of the public activities of this event, I stood inside the Festival and observed the basic transitional contours and cultural structure of Yoruba Traditional Religion, for Ifa is the religion's central dynamic. Within Ifa are the processes and corresponding texts, without which there would be no agency for communicating with the more than 401 (by some accounts over one thousand) orishas in the Yoruba pantheon. All of the orishas and their myriad priests/esses utilize Ifa to help them advise their clients, who are local and overseas.

The homage accorded Ifa by traditional Yoruba is understandable, for they believe that Ifa's knowledge and wisdom transcend time and space and contain the path for ascertaining one's personal destiny and addressing all aspects of the human condition. Thus, the Yoruba consult Ifa on every imaginable subject. Epiphanal moments (birth, death, marriage, travel, change of occupation and business, political decisions, change of residence), illnesses, legal matters, and problems and concerns of every other conceivable type indicate to Yoruba Traditionalists that it is time for Ifa to be consulted in order to restore or maintain harmony in the life of an individual or community.[3]

For centuries, the Yoruba orally handed down to successive generations Ifa texts (*Odu Ifa*) regarding how issues and problems should be addressed. Early in the twentieth century, Yoruba chroniclers began to print verses from these texts, making them more accessible to priests with an Anglophone orientation.[4] Ifa verses contain narratives of the Yoruba's accumulated cultural circumstances and varied problems, with formulaic sacrifices needed to bring resolve. All priests/esses draw from these narratives to call on Ifa. This oracle can be depended upon to function when summoned—even though that is daily, whether observing the Yoruba traditional four-day week or the contemporary seven-day week.

There are similarities between some Ifa and Christian practices, a principal one being that of petitioning the divine. Christians carry their problems and concerns in prayer to Jesus as intercessor between them and God. Ifa is the mouthpiece (intercessor) of the Supreme Being (*Olodumare*). Although Olodumare rarely is directly petitioned to intervene in human affairs, orishas act on behalf of the Supreme Being as emissaries, giving responses to petitions through Ifa textual references. Christians petition through prayer while Yoruba Traditionalists make appeal to the supernatural through divination. Christians, like their Yoruba counterparts, often rely on religious professionals (a priesthood) to help them make intercession with the divine.

Christian priests attend seminaries for training with professors in scripture, history, doctrine, and ritual, while priests/esses of the orishas study divination techniques and texts, rituals, and history with male specialists known as Ifa priests (*babalawo*) and women known as wives of Ifa (*iyanifa*). Christian and Ifa priests learn to use properly the intercessory platforms of their offices, ranging from altars, shrines, and pulpits among Christians to altars, shrines and mats among the Yoruba Traditionalists. Christian ministers, like Ifa priests, also utilize relics and liturgical instruments during their ritualistic petitioning to the supernatural realm. But Protestants, among whom many African Americans and Anglophone-oriented Yorubas of Ile-Ife have contact, frown on the ritual of divination. Although Old Testament scriptures contain acts of divination, Protestants now condemn it as a process that invokes Satan rather than God. They call it a pagan and heathenish act,[5] saying that they rejected it as their religious understanding developed. Consequently, few Christians in the United States have knowledge of or experience with divination, particularly with Ifa divination, so I describe it below in order to lay a foundation for insight into Yoruba Traditional Religion.

The Ifa priestly method of invoking the divine adheres to the following procedure: offering a libation, saying a prayer, and manipulating the *ikin* (palm oil kernels, which some say is the highest order of Ifa divination) or the *opele* (a chain made of skins of the *ope* fruit). The purpose is to derive an Ifa text (Odu Ifa) that addresses problems and concerns. The manipulation of cowry shells functions to derive an Ifa text but is referred to as Merindinlogun divination. Because of their reference to Ifa texts, the priests/esses derive similar results via their diverse methods.

The client of the Ifa priests/esses asks for a divination and sits at the edge of the mat on which the diviner is seated before his wooden divining board (*Opon Ifa*). The diviner proceeds by having the client give her/him an object into which the client whispered her/his concern. The diviner touches that item containing the client's energy to the board, says a prayer while pouring a libation of water, and begins the process of casting *ikin* or the *opele* chain to derive an Odu.

Throughout the process of casting *ikin* or the *opele* chain, the diviner makes four sets of markings. These are written from right to left, moving from top to bottom and are determined by the configurations into which the ikin or opele chain falls. The sets of marks tell the diviner what Odu Ifa pertains to the client's situation. Follow-up questions help the diviner identify the verse that best speaks to the concern. If that text raises questions or is not definitive, the diviner will continue the process while using special effects called *ibo* until a conclusive response is reached. A sacrifice always is required as either propitiation or thanks to the orisha that is mentioned in the Odu as responding to the client's situation. Elegba/Esu is invoked to open the crossroads between this world and the cosmic realm for communication with the orishas. The diviner counsels the client about the situation as addressed by the Odu, including instructions on how to conduct his/her affairs so as to resolve the condition, live with a concern that is irresolvable, or realize that the situation is harmonious. Wherever there are Yoruba Traditionalists divination is pivotal, because Ifa is credited with clarifying or improving the quality of peoples' lives.

Ifa is omnipresent, omniscient, and transnational, extending to Yoruba Traditionalists and other clients wherever they are in the world. Ifa divination extends beyond the Yoruba to the Benin Edo of Nigeria, the Fon of the Republic of Benin (where it is known as Fa), and to the Ewe of Togo (where the system is called Afa). Descendants of enslaved West Africans in Cuba, Brazil, and Haiti still practice it. Ifa is appealed to by adherents and other folks in the United States, Canada, and Western Europe (principally England, France, and the Netherlands) desperate to think that transcendant light can be brought to bear on their concerns. A small group of African Americans in the United States began to address their concerns by practicing Ifa divination in the 1960s, and word of this phenomenon spread from New York City to all parts of the country, eventually being called to my attention in Atlanta.

As with most African Americans, I lived the formative years of my life encountering virtually nothing that was African and being reared in the Baptist Church tradition. In my earliest memories of the 1950s, I recall being baptized along with my elder sister (Nana), singing in the choir, and attending Baptist Training Union and Sunday school. I grew up in two Baptist churches, my father's family church (Reed Street) that was located in the Summer Hill section of Atlanta on Frasier Street. In the late1960s, Reed Street Baptist Church moved to Bankhead Highway and was renamed Paradise Baptist Church. Since my father lived in New York, my mother accepted responsibility for taking her five children to both edifices. But she also took us to the now famous Ebenezer Baptist on Auburn Avenue. Emphasis on prayer, Biblical narratives, baptism by immersion, belief in the Supreme Being and the crucified Jesus, and respect for the pastor as leader of the congregation impressed me. I later discovered that similarities between Yoruba Traditional Religion, and particularly between Ifa and Jesus Christ, are numerous; some of these are pointed out as appropriate throughout the book.

The Christian experience (which also included membership in the Young Men's Christian Association and its summer camp) had a positive and memorable influence in my life. Ebenezer Baptist Church was prominent in that regard. I remember seeing the Reverends Martin Luther King, Senior and Junior, when I was a small boy sitting with my mother and siblings in church. One day I saw my mother's favorite pastor, Dr. Martin Luther King, Jr. on television, leading non-violent protests and being arrested. I was about fourteen years old at the time of Dr. King's incarceration during the Civil Rights Movement in Birmingham, where he spent the longest time in jail and when my mother expressed her grief for him. As a teenager witnessing the racist and unjust brutality directed at Dr. King and other civil rights activists, I told my mother, "I want to help Rev. King!" Her response was always the same, "Okay son, but not until you finish high school." Thus, by observing her respect for Dr. King and her tacit support for my intentions to join the struggle for civil rights as soon as possible, I acquired a sense that one should protest against that which is unjust.

Like the majority of African Americans, I knew nothing about the Yoruba or other African Traditional Religions and had never heard of either Ifa or Ifa Festivals when I had my first encounter with this deity in 1971 at the age of 22. I had dropped out of Clark College (Atlanta) and become a member of the Atlanta-based African Soul Brothers (ASB), an activist organization consisting of a few male students from the Atlanta University Center (AUC), Georgia State University, Atlanta Area Technical Community College and dropouts like me. By later that year my principal work was voluntary, black nationalistic, and Civil Rights Movement oriented, not quite as conventional as my prior job as a fireman.

In 1969, I was the first African American hired at Atlanta's downtown fire station. Firemen were in a civil emergency category, and this gave them gave a modicum of protection from being drafted to go to Vietnam. I nevertheless resented the racism that pervaded the firehouse and dictated the kinds of tasks assigned to me. One daily assignment was for me to clean and shine the boots of other firemen. That was a dreaded task; yet, it paled in the face of a situation in which I found myself when sent to hose a major explosion and fire in a Peachtree Street business. When the smoke cleared, I discovered that during hosing I had been kicking around human limbs and other body parts. My stress reached its limit, and I abruptly quit that job. In the new voluntary capacity with the ASB, I was without draft protection. I soon learned that by quitting the fire station and participating in ASB activities, I had managed to work my way into a tangle with the draft board.

The members of the ASB were eager to honor the memory of both Dr. King and Minister Malcolm X by demonstratively opposing the war in Vietnam. We also proclaimed that as victims of racism, militarism, and economic exploitation, black folk were "colonized Africans" in America.[6] On April 4, 1969,[7] we began to protest these injustices by organizing the Colonized African Vigil on Beckwith Street (in Southwest Atlanta) and reciting excerpts from Dr. King's "Call to Conscience" speech while picketing. In that speech he made an appeal to all young men, but particularly to African American males who were being drafted in large numbers to fight in Vietnam, to file for conscientious objector status. The ASB vowed to honor his appeal by picketing daily against racism, the Vietnam War, and the draft. We took our pickets to the site of the local draft board that then was located on Ponce de Leon Avenue.[8] Our militancy was confrontational.

The African Soul Brothers cultivated an identity that we thought was consistent with the mantras of black cultural nationalism and black power. By the mid-Sixties, African Americans with black consciousness cried out for Black Americans to see themselves as Africans. By 1968-69, the admonitions of Amiri Baraka and Maulana Ron Karenga made inroads among young black males and their nationalistic organizations.[9] The Afro-styles and remember-your-African-roots rhetoric inclined the African Soul Brothers to discard the Anglophone names that we perceived to be relics from slavery, replacing them with names that more appropriately reflected our newly proclaimed Afro images. We had not studied Africa in our schools that offered no such courses, we had not read books on Africa, and most of us knew no Africans. We knew very few African names and nothing about how Africans received names. We gave ourselves first names— Kwaku, Kwesi, and Kofi— that were Ghanaian. These were familiar to us from talking with knowledgeable elders like Bill Ware (an activist with SNCC during its early days and then coordinator of ASB activities).[10] Some of us continued to use our family names; others assumed names that sounded African to us. My full assumed name was, for example, Kofi (Akan, meaning male born on Friday) and Lukwaba Efu (a nondescript substitute for my slave name Louis Eason). After changing our names, we heightened our Afro images by wearing *dashikis* and Afro-styled hair and accessories. We called attention to our right to protest by tauntingly marching in front of the draft board office.

Our challenge to the draft board soon yielded a response. I was among the first ASB to receive a draft notice in late fall 1969. I immediately appealed for conscientious objector status in keeping with Dr. King's "Call to Conscience" speech. At the first hearing, my request for conscientious objector status was passed on for a second hearing. Meanwhile I and the other African Soul Brothers were in and out of jail on charges associated with picketing. While awaiting the second conscientious objector hearing, I received a notice telling me when to report for military duty. I immediately went to the draft board to inform them of their error of not considering that I was waiting to be scheduled for the second hearing. A recruiter told me to go into a room and wait. The room filled with other men, and suddenly everyone there was told to prepare to take the oath for military induction.

I emphatically opposed taking this oath by placing my hands behind my back to be sure that everyone knew that I was not cooperating. The officers instructed us to step forward; I stepped back against the wall. Two military policemen came into the room, placed themselves on each side of me, placed their hands on their weapons, blocked me from leaving the room, turned to me and said, "Yer're in the Army naw, boy!" The recruiters told those who had taken the oath when to report for service. I was taken immediately into custody, handcuffed and whisked away to the military prison at Fort Knox, Kentucky and later to Fort Leonard Wood, Missouri. Thus, I was unlawfully detained and not given the opportunity to complete the conscientious objector appeal process.

Chapter 1

Eventually I was able to get a letter smuggled out to notify my mother of my whereabouts. She alarmed the community. As word of my abduction by the U.S. Military filtered out, my situation became a *cause celebre* in Atlanta and other parts of Georgia. Professor Mack Jones (Ph.D.), a political scientist (who then taught at Atlanta University), and other committed members of Atlanta's Drum Majors for Justice Committee worked with a battery of lawyers and local organizations and churches to free me. I was released but without conclusive hearings on my appeal. I was nineteen and twenty years old at the time, which might help to account for why each time I was released from prison or jail, I went back to join the picket lines and other creative protests only to be arrested again and again by local police.

My militant spirit—fired and stoked by fervor of the Black Cultural Nationalist Movement—inspired me to reject the Baptist Faith. The rejection endured because while I was incarcerated for picketing against the draft, I began to resent the pastor of Reed Street Baptist Church. During a visit to me in jail, he told me to forget about conscience and serve my country by accepting the draft and going to Vietnam. I continued to tell him that I opposed the draft based on the teachings of Dr. Martin Luther King, Jr. who also was Baptist. The Reed Street pastor showed me that he did not have the sensitivity required for counseling me. I was without spiritual counsel for resolving the dissonance caused within me by not having a draft status and being in and out of jail. As my anger toward the pastor increased, my allegiance to the African Soul Brothers deepened.

The 1960s were turbulent times for African Americans who were pursuing racial and economic justice and equality while searching for their Black identity. Much of the inspiration that sustained me during those difficult times came from the prose penned within the group of African Soul Brothers, a form of rap that was sweeping the country. Among these were a pledge and a poem that we recited at vigils and on the picket lines against the background of plaintive, improvisational tones by John Coltrane and the lyrics of Pharaoh Sanders and Leon Thomas.

The pledge had strong motivational dynamic for me as an impressionable young man entering his twenties and seeking solace in a Black identity:

> In the spirit of African brotherhood we pledge a most soulful stand, with our body, mind, sweat and joyful tears; we pledge to exert these energies in the best interest of our People here and in the distant Motherland; we pledge to sleep and waken with spiritual endeavor that will be only in accordance with our ever-growing, liberating struggle; Africa, the blackest star, forever give forth that shining Light! Uhuruh!

The title of the poem—"We Are Africans"—spoke directly to our identity as claimants of African ancestry. The words and cadence of the poem indicates our commitment to our striving for cultural nationalism!

> We are Africans. The time is over for playing;
> The time is now for being.
> No longer will we dance the Watusi,
> In the future we will live the Watusi;
> No longer will we play the Zulu,
> In the future we are the Zulu.
> No longer will we act European, denying Africa;

Chapter 1

> In the future, beginning now, we are what we are—Africans.
> The time is over for playing, the time now is for being!

Our recitations and philosophizing convinced us that liberation was imminent. Our cause was just! The more I was arrested, the more I felt myself to be representative of African Americans and other Third World peoples, all of whom we believed to be colonized by "White" oppressors.

Although I had been released from military detention in early 1970, I was in legal limbo without being given the second draft hearing. I continuously felt threatened by the fact that my case had not been resolved. An avenue toward resolution came through members of the African Soul Brothers.

During the summer of 1971, some of my friends in the Atlanta University Center schools told me that they had heard about an African religious center that might help us to be disentangled from various legal problems. They said that the African-American founder of the Yoruba African Cultural Center outside Beaufort, South Carolina called himself an African traditional priest.[10] He turned out to be Baba Oseijeman (founder and priest-king of the Oyotunji African Village), about whom I write at greater length in Chapter 3. At the time I had absolutely no idea what an African priest or Yoruba person was. My friends had heard it rumored that this priest had a history of helping African-American victims like me to overcome judicial injustices, which I was certain the military action/inaction was. Knowing nothing about the existence of African-American Yorubas, I could not know about the idea of being extricated from legal difficulties by consulting Ifa. During my consultation with Baba Oseijeman about my problems, I first encountered Ifa.

Baba Oseijeman divined for each person in the group of about seven. He used the *Merindinlogun*, a Santeria method that interprets the formations into which cowry shells fall when tossed, giving me my first conscious opportunity to look at sacred cowry shells. He had not yet been initiated to Ifa and did not use the *ikin* or *opele* divination referred to above. He began the divination by pouring a libation of fresh water and reciting a prayer in the Yoruba language. The formations into which the shells fell indicated the Ifa verse that pertained to our respective situations, as he divined for us individually.

Following each divination, Oseijeman carefully explained the details of his findings privately with the individual. He told us that we had problems that had to be resolved spiritually as well as judicially. He told each client about taboos, indicating what we should not do and what we should not eat or drink in order to maintain harmony within our lives. Because of my quick temper, probably the most significant advice to me was that I never should carry knives, guns, or other objects that could be used to injure or destroy life. Use of weapons could cause me not to fulfill my destiny, that is, my predestined potential (*ori*, the life path that the Yoruba believe is seated in the head at birth). For the Yorubas, detecting how one can best pursue or exceed his/her ori is a celebrated aspect of Ifa divination.[11]

From the Odu Ifa, Baba Oseijeman derived Yoruba names for each of us, presenting me with the name Adelade Omoluyi. He explained the name: *Ade* (crown), *lade* (of a crown) or (crown born of nobility arrives), and *Omo* (Child), *luyi* (of his people). From this time, I mixed the names Kofi Lukwaba

Efu and Adelade but still did not legally change my given and family names; an example of this mixing is seen in the *Garvey Voice* article cited in Note 15. After this divination, I felt spiritually reborn and that I had acquired an authentic African identity via the naming. This name heightened my sense of destiny and purpose at one of the most turbulent and critical phases of my young adulthood.

The Odu Ifa derived in my divination was *Odi Ogbe,* an Ifa verse identifying my guardian deity as Oya, goddess of the Niger River, the wind, and protector of ancestral spirits. Figure 1 shows the ciphering for that odu.

Figure 1: *Odi Ogbe*

I	I
I	II
I	II
I	I

Baba Oseijeman explained that Orisha Oya is the female counterpart to the Yoruba God *Shango*, who regulates climatic changes and justice. She parallels the Catholic *Santa Barbara or Joan of Arc*; among the Nile Valley/Egyptian goddesses, she is referred to as *Anubis*.[12] The divination inferred that I eventually would become a priest or devotee of Oya. I seized upon the mention that Oya was also the goddess of change and revolution, for I prided myself on being a revolutionary helping to bring justice to black folk in the United States. As a revolutionary, I needed a supernatural guardian angel.

The divination clarified for me why I was strongly attracted to the civil and human rights movements of the sixties and seventies and to revolutionary ancestors like Malcolm X and Martin Luther King, Jr. Still there was much that I had not learned. For though having attended a high school bearing his name, I knew nothing about the militancy of the African Methodist Episcopal Church Bishop Henry McNeil Turner after whom my high school was named. I later would read about him. It also was in the later Seventies that I learned about Marcus Mosiah Garvey (the pre-eminent Black nationalist leader) and became affiliated with the United Negro Improvement Association-African Communities League. The Ifa experience gave me grounding for an enhanced knowledge of myself as an African Soul Brother, a civil and human rights activist, a follower of Black revolutionary leaders. My confidence in the rightness of having refused to participate in a war that King, Malcolm X and other prominent black and white leaders considered unjust and immoral was strengthened.

During the divination and in his handwritten notes, Baba Oseijeman encouraged me to build an altar to consciously venerate my ancestors and receive spiritual empowerment. He gave me notes summarizing the Odu Ifa and a fascinating diagram of an African ancestral altar. He urged me to erect one and conduct daily meditations. He told me that daily meditation and communion with the Supreme Being, my guardian Orisha Oya, and my ancestors would strengthen and establish my spiritual being so that I would feel less threatened by my legal limbo. Toward this end, I erected my first ancestral altar and began to offer libations and prayers.

By the following year, my daily prayers started out with lighting candles, pouring a libation of water, and chanting this invocation: "*Mojuba Olodumare* (I give praise to the Supreme Being), *Mojuba gbogbo ariku oluwa* (I salute all the lordly ancestors who reside in Heaven)." In the manner of the Oyotunji-Yorubas, I saluted all of my ancestors in this order: those who were buried in the soil of Africa, those who died in the Middle Passage, those whose names no longer are remembered, those recent-dead whose names I remember—including the spiritual ancestors who were African American revolutionaries—proceeding from the longest to the most recently deceased.

The consultation through Ifa, particularly as it related to the resolution of dissonance within me, resembled a Catholic confession. It brought to mind movies I had seen on TV and in theaters where Catholic confessions, if not resulting in immediate resolution of the problem, did bring about within the confessor a feeling of being spiritually cleansed or at the least absolved of a misdeed. The consultation also resembled Catholic confessions in that it centered on a worldview that included a Supreme Being, African saints (orishas), and ancestors. The divination constituted my conscious entry into a deeper awareness of African spirituality and its relation to several aspects of Protestantism and Catholicism.[13] As I became more inclined toward African Traditional spirituality, I learned more about Christianity.

Following the divination, some of my feelings of youthful pride returned. I felt a strong sense of spiritual, physical, and psychological wellbeing. These feelings began to replace the emptiness and loss of respectability that I felt after being arrested. Despite my mother's having said that she was disgraced and having brought her Baptist pastor to try to talk me into renouncing Dr. King's teachings so that I could serve in the military, I now was pleased with myself for being committed to my convictions. The divination allowed me to feel that I was living in harmony with the destiny of a revolutionary spirit that I had received at birth. In spite of this newly found consciousness, I was not extricated formally from my difficulties with the United States Armed Forces until 1977, when President Jimmy Carter declared amnesty for those who had resisted the draft.[14]

By the end of 1971, my association with Yoruba Traditional Religion caused me to cut ties with the African Soul Brothers, which was defunct by the mid-seventies. I was out of jail long enough to become a regular visitor to the Yoruba African Cultural Center, as the pre-Oyotunji community on Brays Island Road then was known. I had met *Kpojito* Omiyale Hwesihuno (who died in March 1979), an elderly priestess to Orisha Yemoja during my first visit while waiting my turn for the divination. She had held the other ASB and me spellbound by telling us fascinating stories about Yoruba Religion and orishas. Dressed entirely in white, the attire of a recent priestly initiate, she had all of the charm and presence of a revered elder along with the persona of a queen mother. I had an affinity for her teaching and drove the approximately six hundred miles round-trip from Atlanta to Brays Island Road twice a week to sit at her feet and hear her talk from the Ifa canon.

My interests in the village and religion extended beyond the affinity that I had for the Kpojito. I hung around so much that I helped with relocating the village from Brays Island Road to its present location. My faithfulness inspired the Chief Elemosha Awolowo to divine for me. Following that divination, he initiated me into the first Egungun Society (ancestral society, *Egbe Egun* of which he was Alaagba or head) of Oyotunji in 1972 so that I could "carry"/wear the *Egungun* cloth (mask). Although I did not know at the time, he was the Oba's first initiate and the first person initiated at one of the South Carolina complexes (Paige's Point Road) that preceded Oyotunji. Our association was close, and Chief Elemosha became diviner for my two small sons until he relocated outside the geographical area. (I gave my sons African names (Kojo '72 and Kwaku '74 and Amansu '83.) Thus, my affiliation with the New Yorubas predated the village's present location and identity as Oyotunji, as is discussed with more detail in Chapters 3 and 5.

The Kpojito relocated to Atlanta and established a temple in 1973, following which I began five years of intense training (1973-1978), under her tutelage, toward preparation for initiation to *Adjakata/ Hevioso*—the Dahomean Vodoun equivalent to the Yoruba's thunder Orisha, *Shango*. I learned the history of Oyotunji and about its early priests/esses. In 1974, I went to New York to live and work with my father, but I missed the spiritual activities and fervent admonitions of the temple. Before leaving, I received sacred implements of *Abesan* (Dahomean equivalent of Oya) and of Yoruba Orishas Esu/Elegba, Ogun, and Shango. While in New York, I longed to know more about Dahomean and Yoruba religions and cultures. This interest led me to the Olatunji Center of African Culture on 125th Street in Harlem. I soon moved into an apartment that the center's founder-director, Nigerian master drummer Babatunde Olatunji, made available to performers. His unique way of immersing aspiring performers in drumming, Yoruba language, songs, and dance unmasked the performance base of the Yoruba culture, as we learned from his enormous repertoire.

I returned to Atlanta in 1976 and was initiated to Adjakata/Hevioso by Medahochi in Gary, Indiana two years later. (He is discussed more in Chapters 3 and 5 as Oyotunji's oldest Shango priest and third initiate of Baba Oseijeman.) This ritual prepared me to receive initiation to Ifa from Medahochi in Gary in 1979 and in 1986 from Baba Oseijeman, who received Ifa in Nigeria. Beginning 1979, I conducted Ifa divinations for clients in Gary and in Atlanta and performed seven initiations in Atlanta.[15] In 1992 my initiations to Ifa by Oyotunji priests were acknowledged in Ile-Ife, when the *Aseda* Awo (Babatunji Adeyefa, number 4 in the hierarchy of the the Awoni—priestly counselors to the Ooni of Ile-Ife) ritually presented me the sixteen *ikin* and other sacred objects of Ifa.

Memories of my years of preparation and praxis flooded my thought during the Ifa Festivals in 1992 and 1999 as I listened to performers reciting Ifa verses, singing orisha songs, playing rhythms, and dancing the steps that characterize the individual orishas. I recalled that my elder brother, Lester Walker, introduced me to LPs of musicians who were popular during the Fifties and early Sixties, while one of my elementary school teachers placed a trombone in my hands and taught me to want to play it when I was in third grade. In high school, I had the privilege of being a disk jockey because I was loquacious and had an impressive enough knowledge of current popular tunes. Being in his native country inclined me to recall during nearly every event how Babatunde Olatunji (who died in 2003) had taught me rhythms and songs nearly twenty years before. He not only had reinforced the foundation for my understanding of ritual music in the Ifa Festivals but also had laid the foundation for my formal studies in music and religion during the 1980s and 1990s at Clark College, at the Interdenominational Theological Center (ITC) in Atlanta, and in ethnomusicology and culture studies at Bowling Green State University (BGSU-Ohio).

This formal study was enhanced by my work with Tyehimba, roughly translating to "We stand as a nation." I learned this word from the Rev. Dr. Roderick McLean (Zimbabwean). As pastor of Delany United Methodist Church in Gary, Indiana, he organized a chapter of the Marcus Garvey's United Negro Improvement Association in 1983, and I became president. While working with him, the word was seared into my psyche. When I organized Tyehimba in 1984 while at Clark College, the word seemed a natural to have Adebayo Bello (Yoruba, Nigeria) and Richard Owens and other African Americans unite to play world music in many forums around Atlanta. These preparations made it possible for me to have informed appreciation for the music of Ifa Festivals.

I also have had satisfying accomplishments in priestly capacities. In 1972-1973, I helped to establish Dahomey Day celebrations in Atlanta under the auspices of the *Ile Mimo* (House of Memories) of Omiyale, who by then had taken the Fon title Kpojito[16]—a point covered in Chapter 3. In 1990 during my studies in African theomusicology in the Master of Arts Program at ITC, I studied and conducted fieldwork on Ifa in Ile-Ife. This paved the way for me to attend and film the Ifa Festival there in 1992 (while a doctoral student at Bowling Green State University); I returned to attend the 1999 Festival. I interfaced dynamics of these festivals with those that I attended and filmed in Oyotunji in 1992 and 1999. In 1993 and 1994, I invited the Aseda Awo and another Ifa priest from Ile-Ife (Adebayo Ogundijo), along with Medachochi and members of his Milwaukee temple to participate in workshops on Egungun rituals, and we established *Egbe Awo*, a society for honoring ancestors. In the summers of 1998 through 2002, I conducted comparative field studies on Ifa and Fa divination under the auspices of *bokonon* (Fa priests) in Cotonou and Ouidah, Republic of Benin.

I had no idea in 1971 that my first visit to the Yoruba African Cultural Center and my first Ifa divination would be the threshold to my journey as a priest of Adjakata/Hevioso, an Ifa priest, and a scholar in African Traditional Religions. My thirty-odd years of personal involvement have given me an opportunity to collect information, experiences, and primary and secondary sources for writing this book. Interactions with Ifa priests (a characterization among Oyotunji Yorubas intended to infer a Fa association as well) in Oyotunji and Ile-Ife and with Fa priests in Ouidah and Cotonou (Republic of Benin) added immeasurably to my understanding and range of experience with divination.

Thus, I take license to write about Ifa from an emic perspective, that is, from the vantage point of an insider and participant-observer. A model for my approach is Karen Brown's *MAMA LOLA: A Vodun Priestess in Brooklyn*.[17] This White, American-born anthropologist has written about Vodou as practiced by Haitian immigrants to the United States and as realized in Haiti. She derived insights and creative license displayed throughout that narrative from her own personal involvement in and study of Vodou. Because I am comparing orisha-based cultures of Ile-Ife and Oyotunji, I have elected to be analytical and descriptive, with a smattering of anecdotal commentary. Throughout this manuscript there is interpretive analysis based on my personal experiences with Ifa rituals, texts, and celebrations in Ile-Ife over a decade and in Oyotunji over more than thirty years.

I have juxtaposed these experiences beside my formal studies, including fieldwork on Ifa, throughout the book. I try not to minimize western concepts and perspectives, hoping to accurately portray the Ile-Ife Yoruba contextual ethos as well as the African American-Yoruba experience.

One aspect of the contextual ethos in Ile-Ife and Oyotunji is sexism. Ifa—in all present-day manifestations—is male dominant. Ifa Festivals are dominated by the Awoni and supported by members of the Ifa priesthood. The Ifa priesthood denies women opportunities to fully participate in rituals and initiation ceremonies. Individual Iyanifa (females trained in Ifa divination and interpretation of Odu Ifa but not fully initiated to Ifa) who have relocated to the United States from Nigeria and those who are in the Oyotunji Movement are beginning to expose and criticize the gendered discrimination. A Jewish woman friend of mine entered these controversial waters when she claimed to have been initiated to Ifa by a Nigerian Ifa priest in New York in 1985.[18] The issue of sexism within the Ifa priesthood as displayed during the Ifa Festivals, along with aspirations of the iyanifa, is examined in historical and contemporary dimensions in several parts of this manuscript. For a priesthood that has a firm tradition of patriarchy, this controversy forebodes change that is threatening.

Recognition of the factor of change in Ifa institutionalism is operative throughout this book. During my liberal arts studies of religious systems at the Interdenominational Theological Center (1988 to 1990), the professors noted that each generation reconstructs and reformulates, i.e., redacts whether consciously or not, what has been passed down from the previous generation. Professors repeatedly counseled us not to accept uncritically definitive interpretations of the

Bible, for example, when handed down as historical fact. They advised us to be mindful of the possibility of each generation's potential for changing, however slightly, tradition and religious documents and interpretations to suit its interests and needs within a particular space of time and geophysical location. I have tried to center myself in this advice throughout this study, as I draw from lived-experiences and the self-stories of the first three generations (myself included) of Oyotunji Ifa priests who have been the pioneers in the Ifa religious reclamation and revitalization movement in North America.

My training in the Ifa priesthood gave me the knowledge and the intellectual and attitudinal base for critical reflection on the Yoruba Traditional Religion. The years of training necessitated that I learn and daily recite and interpret Ifa verses, historical narratives, and traditions while being mindful of how they should be engaged to speak to the African American condition. The creative innovations of Oba Oseijeman and of my godfather, Medahochi Omowale Zannu, are discussed in Chapter 4. Their role-modeling in this regard and my formal studies and praxis prepared me to be able to conduct critical analysis of Ifa culture and the Yoruba Traditional lifestyles throughout this book, from vantage points of my experiences with Ile-Ife and Oyotunji.

A premise guiding my critique of Ifa texts is the understanding that the content of the 256 chapters (Odu), each with hundreds of verses (*ese*) like the Bible and other sacred literatures, has changed over time and space. These texts are transcultural, belonging to the collective memory of Yoruba and New-Yoruba peoples. Some of the seeming contradictions within the texts reflect shifts in political and social history, priestly improvisations, migrations, and

Yoruba cultural diversity and dialectic variation. The linguistic character of the Odu Ifa is archaic, indicating aspects of an aboriginal language that no longer are remembered or used outside the Ifa priesthood. I am mindful that odus are theological and philosophical constructs around which devotees of Ifa center their daily lives and formulate social values and principles. They inform devotees and their clients of their individual and collective destinies and allow them to contemplate ultimate reality and the meaning of life.

I think of the Ifa canon as a mythohistorical literary form, for it is a compendium of narratives about the triumphs and travails of orishas who may be deified ancestors. Speaking specifically of Ile-Ife, I perceive the Ifa texts and mythic narratives to be primary documents that indicate ethnic migrations and other developments in the history of that kingdom, indicating continuity and change of a religious, social, and political nature.[19] Ifa Festivals provided one of the best opportunities for me to detect the relationship between Ile-Ife's actual history and its appropriation of Ifa traditions; interaction between these dynamics offers a panoramic glimpse into important aspects of the city's past. The historical value of the Festivals in this regard, including Oyotunji's improvisations on this Ile-Ife heritage, is treated in Chapters 4 and 5.

Considering the centrality of Ifa in Yoruba Traditional Religion, it is not surprising that there is a sizeable and growing body of published works on Ifa divination and the Ifa literary corpus.[20] I am, nevertheless, not aware of any published studies on the Ifa Festivals in either Ile-Ife or Oyotunji. Dr. Abosede Emanuel wrote an award-winning book on the Ifa Festivals in *Ijo Orunmila Adulawo* (Congregation of Orunmila for Black People) in Lagos.[21] His book is a compendium of information on the worship and celebration of Ifa in that Christian-modeled, congregation, with comparative details from major published studies of Ifa. I know of no published studies comparing the Ifa Festivals in Ile-Ife and Oyotunji.

The most that I have found written on Ifa Festivals in Ile-Ife are a few paragraphs in works by three authors. Bascom's *Ifa Divination* discusses the Festivals of the first eating of new yams by the Ooni and other residents of the palace and first eating of the new yams by the Oluwo and other devotees of Ifa. Wande Abimbola, who was elected Spokesperson and Ambassador for the Yoruba Religion and Culture in the World by the Awoni in 1987, used the example of his native Oyo to discuss the political and religious dimensions of leadership within the cult of Ifa in *Sixteen Great Poems of Ifa*. He is widely known for having been Vice Chancellor of Obafemi Awolowo University in Ile-Ife and for his scholarship on Ifa. The late Chief Michael Ajayi Fabunmi increased my understanding of these Festivals and their significance by placing them within the context of other major festivals in Ile-Ife. The pertinent paragraphs in the books cited above gave me historical compass from which to observe the festivals.[22]

While pertinent paragraphs in the works cited above provided points of reference, most of the information in this book is taken from my emic experiences as an African-American Yoruba and from taped interviews, conversations, handwritten divination notes, and video footage that resulted from my field studies in Ile-Ife and Oyotunji. Video footage—that seems to be the first ever taken of Ifa Festivals in Ile-Ife and the most complete on these Festivals in Oyotunji—has helped me enormously with remembering people and how they participated. This footage helped me to capture the spiritual inten-

Chapter 1

sity and celebrative atmosphere of the festivals during my writing.

In the following pages, I use lenses of culture and history to try to enhance readers' insight into the nature of Yoruba Traditional Religion and the role of Ifa as a mechanism that impacts the private and corporate lives of the priestly devotees and their clients. In Chapter 2, I attempt to make details of the Ifa Festival in Ile-Ife accessible by discussing ways in which that kingdom's early politics influenced continuity and change in Ifa traditions and institutions.

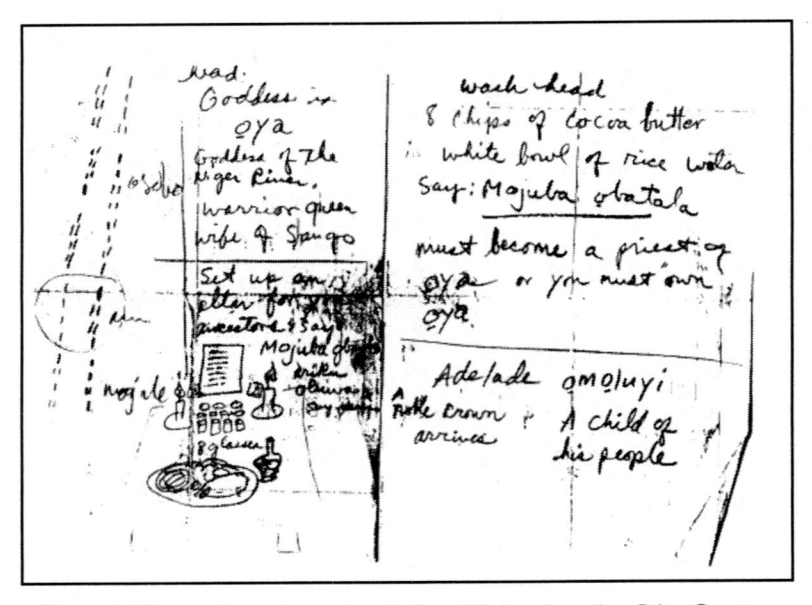

Plate 1: Notes from the writer's first Ifa reading by Oba Oseijeman in the Oba's handwriting, 1971

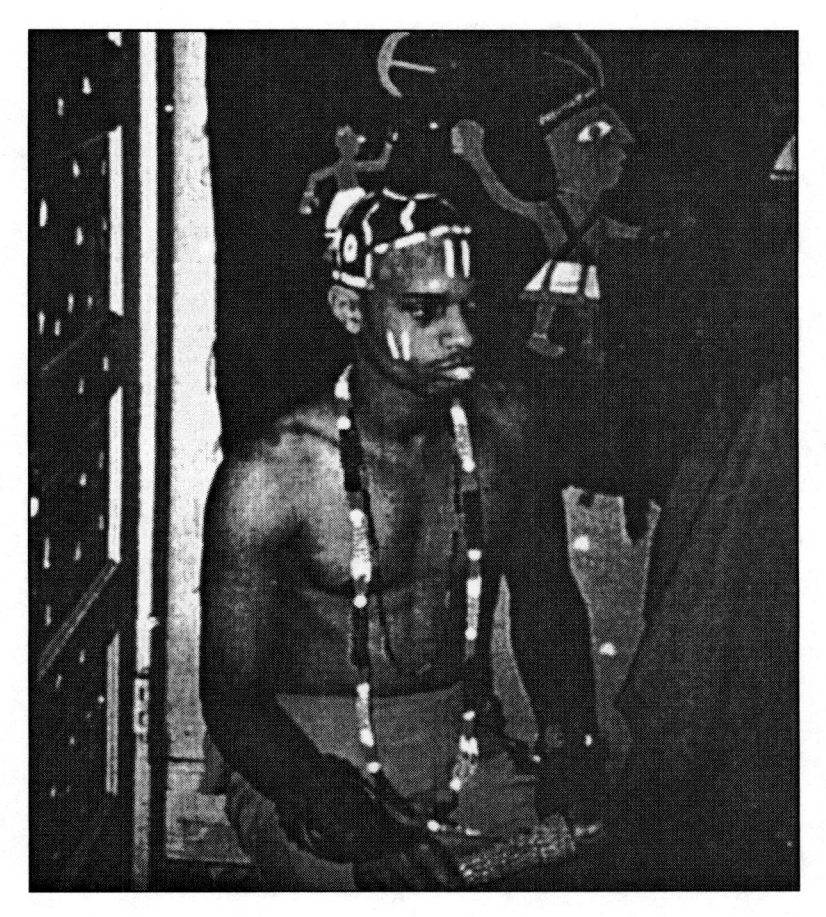

Plate 2: Photograph of the writer at the end of his 1978 initiation to Hevioso

Chapter 1

Plate 3: Oba Oseijeman, *circa* 1971-2, when Oyotunji African Villate was being erected in Sheldon, South Carolina

Notes

1. In "African Kingdom in South Carolina," *SEPIA*, Volume 24, No. 4, April 1975, Milton C. Jordan provides descriptions and a layout of photographs that capture the rustic nature of the village.
2. Margaret Drewal has an interesting discussion of Yoruba ritual as spectacle in *Yoruba Ritual: Performers, Play, Agency* (Bloomington: Indiana University Press, 1992), 13, 15, 205n-206n.
3. Wande Abimbola, *Sixteen Great Poems of Ifa* (UNESCO, 1975), 4.
4. Toyin Falola, *Yoruba Gurus: Indigenous Production of Knowledge in Africa* (Trenton: African World Press, Inc., 1999), 19-20. I have an edition of David Onadele Epega's work cited by Falola.
5. There are several works with this interpretation of Yoruba Traditional Religion; I cite two: S.S. Farrow, *Faith, Fancies, and Fetish, or Yoruba Paganism* (London: Society for the Promotion of Christian Knowledge, 1926) and James Johnson, *Yoruba Heathenism* (Exeter: James Townsend and Son, 1899).

    A book that clarified the unity of purpose among religions of the world for me in the late 1970s was Harold W. Percival, *Thinking and Destiny* (New York: The Word Foundation, Inc. [c. 1974]). His clear explanations on the nature of the universe and the meaning of life was useful to me as one with a Christian rearing when I tried to make sense of African Traditional Religions from my prior Christian perspective.
6. Refer to Dr. King's speech, "Why I Oppose the War in Vietnam," April 4, 1967.
7. See *The Atlanta Voice* Newspaper, June 21, 1970, 3 for an article on the protest.
8. The ASB organization had interests that extended beyond protest, for we also opened and maintained freedom schools in Perry Homes and Vine City (where Beckwith Street is located) and a chess club and cultural arts center on Mason Turner and Hunter Streets, nearby the popular Tibbs Pharmacy and Paschal Brothers' Hotel and Restaurant.

Chapter 1

9. See Clayborne Carson, *In Struggle: SNCC and the Black Awakening of the 1960s* (Cambridge, Mass.: Harvard University Press, 1981) for a reference to Bill Ware.
10. Black Cultural Nationalism and black power and artistic genres, such as rap, that they inspired are summarized in Nell Irvin Painter, *Creating Black Americans* (New York: Oxford University Press, 2007), 324-343. See Carl M. Hunt, *Oyotunji Village: The Yoruba Movement in America* (Washington, D.C.: University Press of America, Inc., 1979), 44-45 and 50-51, for the description of these legal problems.
11. Abimbola, *Sixteen Great Poems of Ifa*, 32-34.
12. Also spoken of in these terms from Brazilian Macumba by Serge Bramly, *Macumba: The Teaching of Maria-Jose, Mother of the Gods*, (New York: St. Martin's Press, 1977), 212; on the Nile Valley goddess, refer to Wallis Budge, *Osiris: and the Egyptian Resurrection*; (New York: Dover Publications, Inc., 1911/1973), Vol. 1, 318-9.
13. Peter J. Paris, *The Spirituality of African Peoples: The Search for a Common Moral Discourse* (Minnesota: Fortress Press, 1995), 22 for a general discussion on African peoples' spirituality and comparisons with Christianity.
14. Stephen M. Koln, *Jailed for Peace* (New York: Praeger Publishers, 1987), 95.
15. Pages of notes written by Djisovi in 1978 and 1979 while he cast Ifa for clients are in available in his files. For article on the Gary Chapter of the UNIA, refer to *Garvey Voice*, November-December 1983, 8. By 1983, I had added Medahochi's assumed African family name, Zanu, following my 1978 initiation.
16. For more information on Dahomean Vodou, refer to Melville J. Herskovits, *Dahomey: An Ancient West African Kingdom* (Evanston: Northwestern University Press, 1967), I & II.
17. Berkeley: University Of California Press, 1991.
18. Experience of Patri Dhaifa are told by her in "Iyanifa: Mother of the Secrets," in *Santeria*, Migene Gonzalez-Wippler New York: Harmony Books, 1989, 110-120.
19. A good background reading on evaluating mythic narratives as history can be found in Thurstin Shaw, "Prehistory of West Africa." In *History of West Africa* 1, ed., J.A.F. Ajayi

and Michael Crowder (New York: Columbia University Press, 1972), 33-77. See also essays in *African Historiographies: What History for Which Africa?* ed., Bogumil Jesiewicki and David Newberry (Beverly Hills: Sage Publications, 1986), 50-110.

20. In addition to William Bascom's very well-known *Ifa Divination: Communications Between Men and Gods in West Africa* (Bloomington: Indiana University Press, 1969/1991) and Wande Abimbola's *Sixteen Great Poems of Ifa* and *Ifa: An Exposition of the Ifa Literary Corpus* (Ibadan, Nigeria: Oxford University Press, 1976), see C. Osamoro Ibie, *IFISM: The Complete Works of Orunmila* (Hong Kong and Lagos, 1986-1993), and S. Solagbade Popoola, *Practical Ifa Divination: Reference Manual for Beginners & Professionals* (1997); Raymond Prince, *Ifa: Yoruba divination and Sacrifice* (Lagos: C.M.S. Bookshop, 1948); and Fela Sowande, *Ifa* (Yaba, Nigeria: Forward Press, 1964).

21. *ODUN-IFA: Ifa Festival* (Lagos: West African Book Publishers Limited, 2000). The name Ijo Orunmila Adulawo is taken from Abimbola, *Sixteen Great Poems of Ifa*, 40.

22. Ifa Divination, 95-99; *Sixteen Great Poems of Ifa*, 6; "Principal Traditional Festivals in Ile-Ife," in *Ife: The Genesis of [the] Yoruba Race* (Ikeja, Lagos, Nigeria: John west Publications, Ltd., 1985), pp. 93-97 but especially p. 95.

Chapter 2

The Oduduwa Influence on Ifa

When I enrolled into Clark College (United Methodist supported) in 1984 and into the Interdenominational Center (ITC)—the preserve of several Protestant denominations—in 1988, my identity as a New Yoruba was palpable. My thinking about Ile-Ife and Ifa continued apace as I studied for the master's degree in African music and theology from 1988-1990. I welcomed courses in critical reflection and dialogue on African Traditional Religions, Judaism, and Christianity. Always the angle for appropriate study was from a cross-cultural perspective. In this formal setting, I sometimes shared my interpretations that developed through the sieve of Ifa mythic literature and priestly counsel from Oyotunji. The mainly Christian-oriented historical and theological discussions by classmates and professors inspired me to think more critically about some narratives that I had been taught from Oyotunji. It was invigorating and disconcerting to be conflicted.

ITC was pivotal in broadening my knowledge of religion and in preparing me for my first travel to Ile-Ife. Just prior to graduation from the Master of Arts program, a telephone call had come to the Atlanta University Center from Emory University asking if anyone would be interested in hosting a babalawo from Ile-Ife. I could not meet him soon enough; it turned out to be Professor Wande Abimbola, whose books on Ifa were introduced to me by Medahochi years before. Oba Oseijeman knew Abimbola, and I had heard him speak of him; the two had met in Ile-Ife, and Abimbola visited Oyotunji. His visit to Emory came just when my wife and I were preparing to travel to Ile-Ife in 1990 for the first time.

Having met him gave me entrée to some of the Awoni and other Ifa priests in Ile-Ife. I arrived there with rapt attention, for while at ITC, I had begun to think more critically about the mythohistories of Ifa and Ile-Ife, comparing them with scientific works. I wanted to learn about the Ile-Ife Yorubas. My studies at ITC, the fortuitous introduction to Abimbola, and the mythic stories of Ile-Ife, Ifa and other orishas, as narrated by Oyotunji priests prepared me to be able to discern fact from inspiration when I arrived in the fabled city.

By some estimates, there are twenty-five million Yoruba-speaking peoples in Nigeria, where they compose about twenty-five separate cultural and political entities. Despite their cultural diversity, they have a number of characteristics in common, two of them being identification with Ile-Ife as a cradle of their civilization and citadel of the worship of the orishas, particularly Ifa.[1] Myths in the Ifa canon that narrate the origins of this city and its people, like the creation stories in the Biblical book of Genesis, have scant documentation for verifying the kingdom's real beginnings. The challenge of being in Ile-Ife and trying to learn Yoruba history was exciting.

The Oduduwa Influence on Ifa

Bolaji Idowu captured the awe inspired in me and among many others claiming a Yoruba traditional identity upon entering Ile-Ife. In *Olodumare,* his book using a Yoruba word for God, Idowu shared memories from his first visit there. He likened Ile-Ife to the Garden of Eden by describing it as, "Ile-Ife: the first [place] of creation here below; the original home of all things; the place from which the day dawns; the enchanted, holy city; the home of divinities and mysterious spirits."[2] This impressionistic statement revealed nothing factual about the kingdom's origins.

Geographical foundations of the primordial Ile-Ife are difficult to establish with certainty. Complicating the matter of location is the fact that Ifa texts mention at least six Ifes: Ife Oodaye (first place of creation), Ife Nleere, Ife Ooyelagbomoro (city of survivors), Ife Wara, Otu Ife (administrative and executive machinery), and the present-day Ile-Ife. The history of all but Ile-Ife occurred so long ago that only the barest material or recorded fragments about them persist. Omotoso Eluyemi observed that without written records and precise archaeological findings, the history is muddled by the myriad of keepers of the cultural narrative. Collectively they have referred to thirteen Ife communities with palaces, royal cemeteries, state festivals, shrines, groves, and lists of rulers (some female, who dropped the title of Oba and became known as Ooni.[3] Without addressing the issue of location, professional and lay historians have surmised that the Ile-Ife in the Ifa myths most likely was not the present-day city.

Based on findings of professional historians who combined oral tradition with scientific research, I have constructed this summary of the origin of Ile-Ife: The most ancient beginnings of Ile-Ife occurred in a deluge or flood, after which the area was begun anew by survivors. Over a period of time, these survivors and/or their descendants assembled themselves into thirteen to sixteen virtually autonomous, family-centered enclaves or lineages that worshipped Orisha Obatala. After the flood, people dwelling nearby—possibly on Ora Hill—invaded Ife. Following their success, the invaders merged the several aboriginal family enclaves into a centralized kingdom under their leadership. The aboriginal enclaves continued to identify with their leader, possibly Obatala. A leader from the invading group became the ruler of Ile-Ife. After a time one of the rulers assumed the name Oduduwa and was heralded as the progenitor of the Yoruba "race." By 1500, Ijebu, Oyo, and several other regional settlements associated themselves with the Oduduwa kingdom and proclaimed Ile-Ife to be the cradle of their civilization.[4]

Historian Babatunde Agiri found remnants of the religion of what may have been the earliest of the Obatala settlers in several Yoruba locations, including Akure in Ekiti State, near Esie in Kwara State, and at Ile-Ife. This finding is supported by anthropological and archaeological studies and suggests that the Oba were the first agrarian people in the area. Palm wine and the eating of the chimpanzees were among their dietary taboos. They worshipped indigenous deities, whose personae are described in the Ifa myths.

According to the mythic narratives, the first settlers were *Irunmoles*, the entities that descended from heaven with or as the orishas and settled in the earth, taking on appearances of humans, animals, natural resources, earth, air, fire, and water. They were the autochthones or starters of cultural development in the region. The autochthones seem to be immortalized in Odu Ifa as having descended to earth in pairs, carrying twice the same name. Thus, Ogbe became Ogbe Meji or twice Ogbe and so on. Among names given them when personified into single identities were Obatala, the orisha of creation, Oduduwa, an earth goddess of successful harvest, and Ogun, the god of iron.

The legend of an invasion from Ora Hill may be based on an historical invading male (group) that became Oduduwa. The legend holds that prior to the first millennium A.D., the deity Oduduwa was a goddess and wife of Obatala, whose name was assumed by the male conqueror. In what must have been an intensely war-like situation, it must have been easier for Oduduwa to assume the name and change the gender of the woman than to take the name of the male, aboriginal leader whom he superceded.[5] In addition to diplomacy, military fiat and demographic assimilation, new regimes among primal peoples authenticated themselves by claiming divinity. The divinity of the male Oduduwa was proclaimed in Ifa orature in a creation story about the origins of Ile-Ife. Here are two of the most common versions of the myths that were told to me in Oyotunji:

> The Supreme Being (Olodumare) sent Oduduwa with a delegation of sixteen elders and followers on a mission from heaven to establish a kingdom on earth. At that time the earth was covered with water. One of . . . [them] brought sand to throw on the water, and a five-fingered fowl spread the sand all over the earth until dry land appeared. To be sure that the earth was firm enough to walk on, a chameleon was sent to test for firmness. Seeing that it was firm, Oduduwa, with the elders and followers, descended onto earth by climbing down a chain onto the land that became known as Ile-Ife.[6]

Heralding this myth was one means of legitimating the conqueroring regime. The Oduduwa conquest claimed validation while denigrating the Obatala contingency and while appropriating some of its traditions.

The second creation myth of the Yoruba that I heard narrated in Oyotunji seems to be from the Oduduwa era. The storyline holds that Olodumare sent Obatala on a mission to earth to create human beings. Obatala drank too much palm wine and made human beings something other than Olodumare wanted them to be. The Supreme Being sent Oduduwa to make the proper people. Thus, the apparently redacted orature held that Oduduwa superseded Obatala as the leader of the peoples of Ile-Ife with the sanction of the Supreme Being.

The word Oduduwa has come to mean *Odu ti o da iwa*, "the great one who creates existence," a statement praising Oduduwa as the mythic hero and progenitor of the Yoruba nation.[7] In a primordial era of women's rights, this name might well have been intended to honor the reproductive capacity of the mother of the settlement. Now it belonged to the male leader of the conquest, the one who replaced Obatala and his wife as procreators of Yoruba peoples. It is fairly certain that repositioning deities within the Ifa orature, separating—for example—the coupled deities Obatala and Oduduwa, could validate the dominance of the invaders. With Obatala labeled as flawed, the name (Oduduwa) of the deity who once had been his wife could be co-opted by the invading leader.

The Oduduwa regime sought legitimacy over the toppled settlers by adopting some of their pre-existing taboos and political protocols. They wove a pre-existing Oba-era taboo into a demeaning rhetoric against Obatala loyalists, declaring them to be flawed from

The Oduduwa Influence on Ifa

drinking too much palm wine. Oduduwa's beaded crown and some prominent deities also may have been continued from the period of Oba traditions. By forbidding subjects to look upon the face of the ruler, Oduduwa must have cultivated deference and submission among his subjects.[8]

Although we do not know the origins of the invaders, they appear to have urged ethnic distinctions based on whether they were indigenes or invaders. Ethnocentric overtones from the Oduduwa phase continue to penetrate Ifa functions in Ile-Ife, as is described in Chapter 4. Ifa scholars essentially agree that the Oduduwa political and militaristic era clearly marked ethnic and gender transformations in the society and collateral redactions in the Ifa canon.

Chief M. A. Fabunmi (a Folk historian), aptly assessed political and social transformations in the Oduduwa era when he alluded to class stratification. The displaced rulers either faded into insignificance or became priests of the various national deities of their people. Thus began the complex process of the dichotomy of functions between the priestly and the ruling classes. In order to securely establish the Oduduwa dynasty and a social hierarchy, the Oonis (the title earlier held by female rulers) transformed the pre-existing class of priests into two divisions—priestly diviners and priestly politicians—for effective governance.

The establishment, if not the beginnings, of Ile-Ife as the cultural homeland of the Yoruba and Ifa are interlocked. According to one account, enclaves formed in Ile-Ife after the flood, had among them two leaders who are remembered in Ifa verses as Obawinrin and Agboniregun (or Setilu alias Orunmila). These verses infer that the Ifa oracle preceded the Ile-Ife of the Oduduwa regime. One of Oduduwa's first official acts was to control the oracle (Ifa) to benefit the new regime. Mythohistory claims that Oduduwa forced Agboniregun (Orunmila) to reside on the hilltop near the Oduduwa settlement in Ile-Ife. This further suggests that the Oduduwa invaders found Orunmila and the Ifa oracle in Ile-Ife when they arrived and determined how they would control the diviners' mysterious powers to their advantage.

One legend, which has been largely discredited, suggests that Orunmila was not aboriginal and came to Ile-Ife from afar. This legend holds that Setilu (Agboniregun/ Orunmila) was a blind diviner who lived in Nupeland (to the North of Ile-Ife) during the first millennium, about the time that the Muslim's began making incursions into Yorubaland. Because the Muslims coveted his skills, they expelled him from Nupe. He fled to the area of today's Benin City (in Edo State) and then to Owo (in Ondo State) and Ado (in Ekiti State); finally Orunmila settled in Ile-Ife, making it his home. The speculation that the Ifa oracle had its beginnings among the Muslims is contested by most Ifa scholars and labeled as a claim by zealous converts to Islam. Abimbola described Ifa divination as "an indigenous African philosophy and thought system . . . that represents the traditional Yoruba world-view." Ifa historian William Bascom found similarly based on analysis of the content of textual references to local vegetation, Yoruba place names, and opposition in Ifa texts to incursions of Islam—in *Odu Otua Meji* for example.

Dr. Abosede Emanuel has provided an interesting twist on the indigenous origin thesis. He analyzes Ifa as a religion that was revealed to the Yoruba in ancient times and refined by the astute teacher Orunmila, who traveled and worked in several Yoruba kingdoms between 500 B.C. and 500 A.D. Thus, he concurs with Abimbola and Bascom on the indigenous origins but speculates further, observing that "the current practice among the Yoruba derives from Orunmila's school which has superseded contending rival schools of earlier times." Emanuel concluded that the last stage in the formation of the divination canon, the affixing "of verses to each of the 256 Odu" was between 500 A.D. and 1400 A.D., a time when all of the major Yoruba kingdoms had been established and their narratives were added.

Some historical accounts place Christianity in Ile-Ife during the period of proliferating Yoruba kingdoms. Shortly after this period of political fecundity, Christianity was eradicated from Ile-Ife according to one chronicler of the kingdom's history. The triumph of Traditionalism over Christianity was remembered in the Itapa Festival that feted Obatala.[9] Until more research settles the issue of Christianity's presence in Ile-Ife, one can only wonder if and how Christianity influenced Yoruba Traditional Religion and the Ifa canon in that pre-colonial era.

Professor Wande Abimbola has commented that one myth places Ifa's birth at Ile-Ife and says he was a skillful medical man and diviner who later became king (*Alaketu*) of Ipetu. He became popular and taught people from across Yorubaland to divine and chose sixteen of them to be his disciples. This narrative holds that a memorial to these priests is preserved in the names of the sixteen primary Odu of Ifa.[10] Abimbola makes no distinction between Orunmila the deity and Ifa the oracle. He comments that, "Ifa is believed [by Yoruba Traditionalists] to be one of the major divinities who descended from heaven [*orun*] into the settlement of Ife by means of an iron chain."[11] Iron production in the vicinity of Ile-Ife dates from about 500 B.C. It is Abimbola's opinion that Ifa verses associating the diviner's emergence in the town with an iron chain and a cutlass are markers pointing to an actual historical context. The suggestion is that not only Ifa but also ikin first came to Ile-Ife.

Explaining the circumstances under which Orunmila gave the sacred palm nuts to followers in Ile-Ife, Abimbola recounted the following,

> Orunmila stayed at Ile-Ife while other divinities went to other cities; Eshu/Elegba went to Ketu, Ogun to Saki, Orishanla to Ifon, etc. By some accounts, Orunmila spent some time in the Ado section of Ile-Ife, marrying many wives and raising eight sons whom he taught, along with some friends, the secrets of Ifa divination. After a time, Orunmila returned to heaven following an insult from his youngest son. While he was gone, chaos broke out. When Orunmila's children tried to bring him back to earth to help restore peace, he refused to return. They went to heaven to beg their father to return.
>
> In his place, he gave each one of his children the sacred sixteen palm nuts, which became, since then, the most important symbol of Ifa divination.[12]

In other words, the vacuum created by the absence of Orunmila was filled by his gift of sixteen palm nuts and the science, ritual, artistry, and literary system associated with it.

On the issue of Ifa's origins, nevertheless, we are left with a question, in any mythic event, that cannot be definitively answered. Believers are satisfied that Ifa divination has been in Ile-Ife for a very long time and that it has superhuman qualities and divine origins. They are more interested in making use of it than in quibbling over its origins.

Ifa priests and their clients praise and celebrate Ifa. Abimbola has stated that in addition to Ifa and Orunmila, this orisha has several names and praise titles. "He is known as *Afedefeyo* (master of the Oyo dialect as well as other languages); and *Akerefinusogbon* (the small man with a mind full of wisdom)...; [and] by the revealing name *Obarisa* (king of the divinities)." Dr. Obosede Emanuel lists several additional names for Ifa/Orunmila: "*Ela* ("Savior or Redeemer", suggesting here the Christian influence in Ijo Orunmila). Among other praise and descriptive names for Ifa are *Agbonmiregun*, *Edu* ("Black One in reference to his symbol, the black palm-nuts"), *Bara-Petu* (Lord of Ipetu, a city reputed to have been founded by Ifa"), *Ara Ado, Ara-Owo, Ara-Ibini* (because Ifa traveled to or lived in these cities), *Baba-L'exin-Oye* (Royalty of the city Oye, a locale in Ekiti), *Opitan Olufe* (Historian of or from Ife).[13] Apart from these names, Ifa is variously described.

Ifa is a canon of divine wisdom and knowledge made accessible to humans for maintaining harmony on earth via divination. As a repository of Yoruba traditional knowledge, Ifa is useful for addressing all human concerns. Ifa is an archive with narrative accounts of Creation, the activities and problems of the orishas and deified ancestors, and historical events. The Ifa literary canon contains markers to Yoruba history, accounts of orishas's personal lives, the Yoruba traditional worldview, procedures for conducting rituals and ceremonies for every conceivable occasion, formulae for resolving individual and civic problems, prescribed sacrifices, prescriptions for healing, poetry, and songs and chants.[14]

The Yoruba worldview that gave rise to the Ifa system is enveloped in the Yoruba concept of *ashé* (divine energy), a metaphysical principle indicating that an entity has energy or power to get things done. Although Eshu/Elegba is believed to be responsible for keeping ashé, this power emanates from the Supreme Being and permeates all matter in the universe. It is ashé that allows divinities and humans to communicate. For the Ifa diviner, ashé is a practical and immediately accessible phenomenon that energizes their divining instruments, including the air around them. The use of ashé in harnessing and activating the cosmic energy that is believed to reside in all animals, plants, hills/soil, rivers, human beings is identified closely with detecting problems and healing.[15]

The supernatural element in ashé may be illustrated with reference to the philosophical concept of *ohun* (verbalization or sacred performance of the word). A familiar example to Jews, Christians, and Muslims is seen in God's calling forth creation in the Biblical Genesis narrative. If we regard ashé as a universal force, ohun is the benevolent, procreative voice, while *epe* is malevolent. This duality signifies the law of opposites (good and evil, procreative and destructive) that when balanced allows harmony to be maintained and/or re-established.[16] Ashé acts like a fulcrum during divination, for it is the path for communication between the orishas and humans via Elegba/Eshu—who sits at the top of the divining board—mediating communication between gods and humans.

It is impossible to appreciate Ifa divination without exposure to the ritual. Ifa divinations are conducted by Ifa priests, who during the procedure, write the message(s) from the Supreme Being and the deities(s) in esoteric cryptograph on rectangular or circular ceremonially-carved, wooden trays *(Opon Ifa)* that are sprinkled with wood powder or meal (*iyerosun*). Ifa priests energize the board for Ifa's entry into the divination process by tapping on the Eshu/Elegba figure, which generally is in the center top of the divining tray, with an instrument called *iroké*. In one hand, the diviner holds sixteen Ifa palm nuts taken from the palm tree known as *ope Ifa* (Ifa's sacred palm tree, mentioned in a creation myth above). These palm nuts have four indentations, suggesting a head with eyes, a nose, and a mouth.[17] After being ritualized for divination, Ifa the sacral palm kernels are called ikin. As previously stated in the "Introduction," Ifa divination is also commonly performed with chains.[18] Yoruba Traditionalists think, however, that ikin divination is the more accurate and powerful means of accessing divine knowledge.

There is an ordered procedure for using *ikin* to derive an Odu Ifa. During divination with palm nuts, the priest holds the *ikin* in one hand and cups the other hand over the *ikin* to gather them up until only one or two remain. When two *ikin* are left in the hand, one vertical line is marked. The markings are written from right to left, as marked in Figure 1, to obtain the number for the Ifa verse that addresses the client's problem or concern. When one *ikin* is left, two single vertical lines are drawn close together on one side of the divining board, as marked in Figure 2. This procedure of making one or two marks is repeated until eight sets of markings (often a mix of one and two straight lines, as shown in Figure 3) have been recorded. Examples of the set of eight markings and the sequence of making the markings (moving from bottom to top and left to right) are seen in illustrations 1 – 3.

Chapter 2

Figure 1: *Odu Ogbe Meji*

I(2)	I(1)
I(4)	I(3)
I(6)	I(5)
I(8)	I(7)

Eight single vertical lines indicate that the diviner had 4 sets of two ikin left in his hand during the process. The configuration in Figure 1 signifies the name of the first major Odu Ifa, *Ogbe Meji*. This Odu is said to be the mother of the remaining major fifteen Odu. When the reverse occurs and only one ikin remains in the hand eight times, two vertical lines are marked, forming the second major Odu Ifa—*Oyeku Meji*; its esoteric cryptograph is illustrated in Figure 2.

Figure 2: *Odu Oyeku Meji*

II(2)	II(1)
II(4)	II(3)
II(6)	II(5)
II(8)	II(7)

A series of tries that leave a mix of one and two *ikin* in the hand eight times has a mixed pattern such as that in Figure 3.

Figure 3: *Odu Ose Ika*

II(2)	I(1)
I(4)	II(3)
II(6)	I(5)

II(8)   II(7)

Once the process is completed, the priest may be directed by the Odu to repeat another series that will yield another Odu as an answer or question to the original one. When the procedure is complete, the diviner begins to recite, and if pertinent, sings verses of the Odu derived from the divination. Many Odu Ifa contain songs and sometimes a dance or other sacred movement and rhythm.

Why does Ifa know so much and how can Ifa resolve so many problems with the ceremonial ritual of divination? We now know that Ifa is trans-generationally accumulated knowledge and history of traditional Ile-Ife. The canon containing this knowledge and history is attributed to one deified individual—Ifa. This deity obtained his store of knowledge because he was the only orisha present with Olodumare during the process of Creation.[19] Thus, Ifa carries the title *Eleri Ipin*, "witness at Creation," implying that Ifa knows the future of all things as well as their past. Thus, the Ifa Traditionalists of Ile-Ife declare that Ifa is second only to Olodumare in knowledge and wisdom.

Ifa is believed to have been present at Creation and is credited with knowing the nature of the entire universe and its workings. Therefore, he is uniquely equipped with knowledge and skills necessary for restoring order where there is confusion and chaos. Ifa is said to be able to bring certainty to uncertainty while restoring hope to the hopeless and peace between warriors. The lyrics of one Yoruba song memorialize the power of Ifa:

> E e wohun ti 'Fa'n se;
> E e wohun ti 'Fa'n se;

> Ifa lo sabala di kaa;
> E e wohun ti 'Fa'n se.
> Come, come look at what Ifa has done.
> Come, come look at what Ifa has done.
> Ifa has turned a barren land into a palace.
> Come, come look at what Ifa has done.[20]

By being present at Creation, Ifa has the advantage of knowing destiny and how it will impact everyone and all things, including the gods, ancestors, spirits, humans, animals, plants, rocks, rivers, and the spoken words of songs, prayers, praises, curses. An Ifa chant speaks to this range of knowledge and authority acquired at Creation:

> Ifa lo loni;
> Ifa lo lola,
> Ifa lo lotunla pelu e,
> Orunmila lo nijo mereerin Oosa daaye!
> Ifa is the master of today;
> Ifa is the master of tomorrow;
> Ifa is the master of the day after tomorrow;
> To Ifa belong all the four days
> Created by Oosa on earth.[21]

A feature of historical knowledge is that it may be perceived as a predictor of future trends in the lives of individuals and communities. Ifa always is consulted before a major event occurs in one's life or whenever a rite of passage is performed, i.e., birth of a child, marriage, when a chief is being installed, or at funeral rites in order to try to read the past into the present and future. Retired Obafemi Awolowo University Professor 'Bade Ajuwon (who specialized in African Traditional Religions, Sacred Literatures, and Languages) alluded to this feature in a discussion of predestination in one of his works. He stated that

Ifa texts provide a basis for understanding the Yoruba theo-philosophy of predestination. He simplified his statement with this explanation:

> The idea that a person dies from an accident, becomes a millionaire, fails an examination, is placed in slavery, is loved by many, runs amuck, or possesses great skills and talents, all are traceable to one's predetermined destiny and revealed through Ifa divination generally after the fact. Some readings precede the fact and are derived in part from knowledge of tradition, for example an infant ... [is declared] to be destined for a particular vocation based on the vocations and titles and positions held by the parents.[22]

The vastness and omnipresence of Ifa is noted in the idea that Ifa is the only Yoruba divinity understood to be the mouthpiece of both the Supreme Being and all other divinities.[23] Ifa knows when an orisha is angry with or wants the attention of an individual or community. Ifa is assisted by Esu (Elegba), who manipulates ashé in order to permit communication between people and orishas. Being the intermediary between orishas and humans, Eshu heralds the message to the deities after assuring that the appropriate sacrifices have been made.[24] These priests who access the sacred wisdom are called babalawos (fathers of Ifa mysteries). Ifa priests earn respect and confidence because of their abilities to address meaningfully social, psychological, physical, and spiritual disorders and concerns.[25]

Training for Ifa priests is lengthy. They sometimes start training with a master babalawo before age ten. The training normally lasts between ten and fifteen years; this of course depends on the age at which one starts training and one's eagerness and ability to learn. Before mastering *ikin*, the trainee must learn to use the *opele*. This first level is known as "*sisi opele je* [a short form of Ifa divination that employs the Ifa divining chain]."[26] Along with mastering the art of divination with the *opele*, a trainee's preparation involves the memorization of several of the two hundred and fifty-six Odu.

The process of learning Odu verses begins with memorizing the first and most important Odu, *Ogbe Meji*.[27] Apprentices learn one or two verses at a time, "parroting their *oluwo*" (teachers with a number of initiates attached to her/him).[28] The enormity of this task was estimated in Albert McGee's essay, "Mathematical Observations on Ifa." He explained that if the trainee learns two "ese Ifa in each Odu, then he will know a total of 2 X 256 = 512. . . . If he learns four, he will know 4 X 256 = 1024" and so on.[29] This process allows the trainee to gain self-confidence and control over the symbiosis of Ifa sacred arts and skills in the Ifa canon, including history and political protocol, medicine and other sciences, dances and chants/prayers, arts and crafts.

An example of a complex of skills required in a formula for healing is found in a verse from *Odu Ogbe Meji*:

> Orunmila says we should sigh "hin;"
> I say we should take a breath and rest;
> He says that the one who sacrifices water will have a breathing spell.
> Orunmila says we should sigh "hin;"
> I say we should take a breath and rest;
> He says that the one who sacrifices ochra will have honor.
> Orunmila says we should sigh "hin;"

> I say we should take a breath and rest;
> He says that the one who sacrifices salt will find satisfaction in his affairs.
> One calabash of cold water is required.
> We will pour salt into it; We will slice ochra into it also.
> We will mark *Eji Ogbe* in the divining powder;
> We will add the divining powder to the water also.
> The person for whom this figure was cast will drink of the water[y mixture],
> And anyone else who wishes may drink of it also.
> Afterwards we will pour whatever is left at the base of Esu.
> Ifa says that the person for whom we cast this figure wants a breathing spell;
> He will get a breathing spell, and will gain honor also.[30]

This example illustrates the performative and healing nature of prescribed sounds (*hin* above, for example) in divination verses. It infers that cryptic messages and instructions for appeasing designated orishas are contained within the verse. The same Odu requires participation of the client and invites on-lookers to take part. Interpretational skills and visual and aural discernment are required of the priest, indicating the vast base of knowledge that the diviner is expected to master.

Ifa trainees soon determine that divination verses have structure/order—an introductory phrase, a statement of the problem, the sacrifice for correcting the problem. The babalawo begins the oracular statement with a little drama when using the word "hin," as in sighing. Then he states the problem; the above verse, for example, indicates that the person needs a rest. Next the babalawo announces the sacrifice that is needed: cold water (indicating that in order to fetch water, one has to take a break from all other activities), salt (that brings savor to the situation as salt seasons food), and sliced ochra (that signifies the bringing of honor). The diviner has learned that the sacrificial elements, including time from work are required for this particular client's healing in accordance with this verse of this Odu Ifa. In order for the divination to have its intended impact, the mandated structure and required elements must be adhered to.

In addition to mastering several of the two hundred and fifty-six major and minor Odu, initiates to the Ifa priesthood are required to know and perform the sacrifices inherent within each Odu. Once mastering a number of the Odu Ifa the trainee proceeds to learn analysis and interpretation. Without proper instruction in these skills, one can neither hear oracle nor communicate meaningfully the oracle's message to clients. The clients seek out diviners who can discern the message from the oracle and offer the sacrifices necessary to resolve the problem.

After the initiate has ascertained the necessary level of knowledge and discretion according to the *oluwo*, members of the Ifa priesthood from neighboring towns, cities, states, and even countries are invited to the appropriate portions of the initiation ceremonies. These public ceremonies include feasting, drumming, singing, dancing, and chanting Ifa orature.

As in western professions, upgrading is a life-long process. The initial training provides only a foundation, which will allow one to practice at primary levels. Trainees at the basic levels understand that they must pursue a field of focused knowledge in order to become a specialist. It was through specialized training that Ifa priests in Yoruba traditional societies become revered physicians, supporters of midwifery, psychiatrists, surgeons, counselors, mediators, judges, and exorcists upon whom the community relied. In traditional Ile-Ife, some of them even played political roles of spying and peace-keeping as required by the Oduduwa dynasty.[31]

The highest level of Ifa priesthood in Ile-Ife is that of Awoni—advisers to the Ooni; they have dress and/or ornaments that give them distinction from other Ifa priests. I summarize my observations of them on the formal occasion of the Ifa Festival with an account from William Bascom to describe traditional aspects of their dress. They wear, or at least own, a red tail-feather from the African gray parrot, tucking it into the band of their western-styled hats. They wear a bracelet of tan and green or green and gold beads. Some wear beads flung over one shoulder and across the chest, although all receive these beads in Awoni installation ceremonies. They carry a whisk made of ram's hair while wearing Yoruba-styled garments of their choice. They have passwords, one of which (*"Ogbedu"*) is used during Ifa divination.[32]

In the traditional past, the attire of the Awoni was distinct from that of other Ifa priests, who acknowledged the superiority by doffing their hats and prostrating (or bowing from the waiste) before them when meeting on the street. These Awoni may have had these accouterments with them at all times in the past, but in contemporary times, they just as often may not. I have seen some who look as though they are determined to adhere to tradition in their appearance and others who are not so inclined. In modern times, requirements of secular work and commerce, travel, and professional careers incline the Awoni to be less tradition bound except during ceremonial occasions.[33]

The Awoni are honored as the most knowledgeable of all Ifa priests in Ile-Ife. The size of this council reflects on the importance of the number sixteen in the Yoruba philosophical system that is based on the sixteen major Odu. William Bascom ranks positions within the Awoni in this order: Araba, Agbonbon, Agesinyowa, Aseda, Akoda, Amosun, Afedigba, Adifolu, Obakin, Olori Iharefa, Lodagba, Jolofinpe, Megbon, Tedimole, Erinmi, Elesi. Their titles are kept for life unless one becomes Araba or Agbonbon. The position of Araba is generally accepted as being reserved for babalawos from Oke-Itase (where trusted advisers to Oduduwa are believed to have lived during that dynastic era) although some have been elected from other compounds in Ile-Ife. The Awoni are elected to their respective offices by their peers based on eligibility requirements. They must be native-born males and practicing babalawo, who received *Olodu* (Odu, a ceremonial pot used in the initiation of Ifa priests).[34]

The Awoni and/or its individual members are obligated to divine for the Ooni whenever he submits a request to them. This obligation is a convention from the time of the Oduduwa conquest, when the priestly tasks were separated from the kingship and the priestly function was mandated to serve the political interests of the crown. The Ooni may ask the Awoni to divine for the town, although today their findings are not binding on the secular arena. Divination for the town occurs when there has been trouble that touches a large number of people or when there has been a troubling dream or other omen brought to the attention of the Ooni. On ceremonial occasions at least, divinations requested by the Ooni are performed in the palace's Ifa shrine. During these palace rituals, the Awoni use the Ooni's divining apparatus.[35]

Despite the fact that the offices of the Awoni are restricted to males and initiation into the Ifa priesthood is denied women, Ifa verses are abundant with divine wisdom as a female principle. These texts are likely to be remnants of the pre-Oduduwa civilization, a more mother rights-centered dispensation.[36] Odu *Osa Meji* tells us, for example, that Odu (the nuggets of wisdom) came to the autochthonous people of Ile-Ife in a female persona. Verses in the Ifa canon state that Olodumare sent three supernatural beings: Ogun, Obarisa, and Odu to the world *(aiye)* in order to make earth habitable. Ironically Odu was the only female among the three emissaries from the Supreme Beings. All had skills: Ogun knew the science of metallurgy (technology) and had the power to be victorious in battle. Ogun's power is symbolized in the machete, gun, sword, and all other metal objects. Obarisa had the power to create and destroy people. Odu's purpose for being on earth was unknown initially and not revealed until she returned to Olodumare to inquire about her destiny. Ogun and Obarisa never returned to visit Olodumare.

As a result of Odu's returning, Olodumare made Odu chief of all the divinities and bestowed upon her power to keep earth from self-destructing. Olodumare asked Odu how she would use the power given her when she returned to earth, and she responded thusly. Upon arriving on earth, she would war against all those who would not listen to Olodumare. She would give wealth and children to those who asked. If she granted someone's wish and that person became impertinent and disrespectful to her, she would take the wealth and children back. Olodumare said this is good, but cautioned Odu to use her powers with extreme calm and good will.

Accordingly Olodumare told Odu that if she used her powers for evil or violence, he would reclaim them. Olodumare then declared that all human beings must follow Odu in order to live harmoniously. Odu was all that was wise, knowledgeable, and virtuous. Humans would live by the edicts of Odu until the other emissaries (by my guess Ifa priests of the Oduduwa era) declared in *Owonrin Meji* that she had lost her authority and knowledge to Ifa for being cruel.[37] Although Ifa scholars seem to have virtually no interest in writing about what must have been a revolt against mother rights, sexism and its origins in the Ifa priesthood concerns pan-humanists. The patriarchal revolution seems to have been systemic, for Oshun—deity of fertility, creativity, and Merindinlogun, suffered a similar fate among diviners.

Oshun was one of the orishas sent by Olodumare to organize the world according to *Odu OseTura*. She initially was honored by Olodumare and given the powers of divination and sent to organize earth. She was the only woman, and the male orishas discriminated against her. They left her out of their meetings on earth, and she obstructed their plans. They reported this to Olodumare, who told them to apologize and make a sacrifice to her. Oshun told them "that she wanted ... [all] of the ritual[s] they perform for men which they used to keep women behind, ... And she wanted every woman who is powerful like her to be initiated. So they called Oshun, and they showed her everything." That "everything" turned out to be Merindinlogun divination. This indicates, I think, a transformation or addition to the primal system. We do not know if it was the original tool of divination.

Presently however in Ile-Ife, it is identified with the assistant to Ifa.

In a later Odu (*Okanran Sode*), the mythmakers explained why Oshun lost control of divination. They said that she refused to make the sacrifice that Olodumare commanded and lost control over knowledge to her husband, Orunmila. In other Ifa verses, there are variations on these narratives that rationalize Oshun's loss of authority, all suggesting redactions away from her primordial role and image.[38] A myth found among the Edo of Benin City (Nigeria) focuses on their deity Arugba. The primal role of Arugba and her descent are so strikingly similar to Oshun's that I have placed it in the Appendix for your benefit.

These Ifa narratives on Odu and Oshun provided a rationale for the devolution of women's priestly and political authority in Ile-Ife, for they signified that women's loss resulted from disobedience to Olodumare or abuse of power. The images of the female orisha in these Odu Ifa not only suggest redaction within the text, but they indicate also that women's social authority was debased. Historian Biodun Adediran emphatically made the point that women once ruled a number of Yoruba kingdoms prior to the Oduduwa dispensation. He argued that legends in western parts of Yorubaland suggest that the society was matrilineal, and sometimes matriarchal, and that as recently as 1600 to 1889 women were not subjugated to their male counterparts.[39]

It may be that women crafted marketwomanry into a new base of self-affirmation and empowerment following the loss of their former roles as rulers and principal Ifa diviners. In Ile-Ife, the patriarchy (supported by redactions in Ifa texts and interpretations by Ifa priests headed by the Awoni) apparently reacted by portraying the marketplace as the locale of trickery and evil, necessitating the placement of a patrol of masculine forces, i. e. Ifa diviners and members of Egungun and Oro societies.

Obviously the patriarchy was trying to curtail the power of women who did not submit to the arbitrary authority of patriarchal forces.[40] Consequently the patriarchy used the Odu Ifa to justify males having superseded females in authority. Women's authority was so weakened that even one side of the Odu Ifa (the right and believed to be the more powerful) is declared by Ifa priests to be male. These mythic scenarios suggest that women diviners (symbolized by Odu and Oshun) were banned from rights in the Ifa priesthood, except as assistants to babalawos. The priests refuse to fully initiate them into the priesthood.

In the "Introduction," I mentioned the denial that Dhaifa, the Jewish woman who asked to be initiated to Ifa, experienced following rites staged by an Ifa priest from Nigeria. He denied that he had given her the full initiation. Nigerian women complain as well. Mrs. Jokootifa Ayoka Ajanaku-Scott, daughter of the late Ifa Chief Priest in Lagos, has spoken eloquently about this discrimination that parallels experiences of women in Ile-Ife and elsewhere in Yoruba societies.

Her father initiated her into the Ifa cult in 1960 so that she could assist him when he initiated Ifa priests. The Odu received during her initiation to Ifa was *Ogbe Meji*. Adherents of Ifa believe that this Odu is the most powerful of all of the two hundred and fifty-six major and minor Odu Ifa. I would add that often a person initiated to Ifa under *Odu Ogbe Meji* is thought to be among the most spiritually endowed with the greatest potential imaginable for possessing mystical powers. These persons are considered to be powerful ambassadors of Ifa.

Unlike their reactions to youthful Yoruba males initiated to Ifa, the Ifa priests forbade Ajanaku-Scott to see "Odu,"[41] basing their decision on Odu *Ofun Meji*. The reference here is to the fact that males are taken to Olodu (a grove for initiations to and ceremonies of the Ifa priesthood—babalawos), their ikin are prepared for divinations for that priest throughout his life, the ikin are cast during the initiation ritual to ascertain the Odu that will guide his life—an Odu that only can be derived by using the specially prepared ikin. Women cannot go into the grove and cannot observe Odu being derived in this ritualized way.

Margaret Drewal made a reasonable conjecture about how this discrimination is continued:

> The reason most often given for . . . [gendered] divisions . . . involve perceived differences in the natures of men and women. It is considered more fitting for men to work in hard materials and for women to use soft ones. By extension, men work with iron tools that require direct, forceful action—striking slashing, hammering, or even "beating," as in the process of palm-nut divination."[42]

These notions help to relegate women diviners to the Merindinlogun system.

The babalawos say that *Odu Ofun Meji* directs them to isolate women diviners, claiming that this verse speaks to the presence of very strong medicine (women's menstruation) that may threaten the safety of babalawos. This is based on the myth that Ofun Meji was the last Odu to return from Heaven to meet with Ogbe Meji and so was rejected by all of the other Odu and not permitted to join in the feast with the

Odu. The other Odu told Ofun Meji that its place among the Odu would be last. Ofun Meji protested and put up a protracted struggle against all of the other Odu but never faired well. Women priests of Ifa are associated with the allusion to strong medicine in Odu *Ofun Meji*, referring no doubt to menstruation, making women too powerful to be fully admitted to the Ifa priesthood during those years and presumably after the onset of menopause since no iyanifas are permitted to see Odu.

The males in the Ifa priesthood, therefore, established a policy and continue to use it against women, despite the likelihood the female gendered were the initial givers of Odu. This policy is all the more perplexing when related to the plights of Odu and Oshun, who had received full priestly authority from Olodumare but later were discredited in Ifa verses.[43] Contemporary literature indicates that roles and opportunities for women as priests in the Ifa cult are politically constructed by the male authorities. One wonders how cognizant male, Yoruba scholars are of the limitations placed on women by cult leaders when they write that,

> Women can also be members of the cult and can be initiated as priestesses of Ifa but in most cases, there are very few women who can undertake the long years of training demanded as a yardstick for initiation. This is due mainly to the demands of marital and parental life on women. However, there are a few important women [wives of babalawos and apetibis] in every community who take active part in the activities of the cult.[44]

Isn't it likely that few women join the Ifa cult because of the mortifying insults they are expected to endure as second-class members? When confronted with responsibilities of wife, mother and daughter in addition, they must think to themselves, "Why bother?"

Even the word "babalawo," that identifies the Ifa priesthood, is rooted in the Yoruba masculine term "baba," "father." I will repeat the fact that the cryptographs of Odu are written in two columns—right (male and strong) and left (female and weak). Bascom reminded us that "for this reason, the name of the right half precedes that of the left."[45] The question begging to be raised and answered here is whether there is something structural in Ifa thought that made the system vulnerable to sexism and that makes sexism sustainable despite the "affirmation of [gender] complementarity" that is inherent in the divination system. Philip Peek, who has written about divination in Africa, noted that "complementarity, . . . is a key dynamic in [Ifa] divination and depends on interaction of male and female halves."[46] This concept indicates that there is provision in Yoruba history, worldview, and the Ifa literary corpus for rethinking and transforming the Ifa priesthood in ways that will have positive gendered impact on society.

Adediran has aptly remarked that, "In spite of limitations to the political power of women in some Yoruba kingdoms, their preeminence during primal stages of development is evident in traditions and rituals connected with the founding of these kingdoms." Jacob Olupona wrote along the same lines about the Ondo-Yoruba. The Ondo throne was established by a female or by a dynasty headed by women. After being forced to renounce the throne following the circulation of unflattering comments about her by male councilors, the woman ruler named and installed her male successor before relinquishing the crown.[47]

A similar tradition suggesting gendered altruism is displayed in the annual Itapa festival, a religious event honoring Obatala and his wife (Oduduwa) by carrying them in stone effigy to the area in which they are believed to have lived in Ile-Ife. This festival suggests the importance of this female deity in the founding of Ile-Ife in the pre-Ooni Oduduwa era. It infers that this wife possessed a powerful political image that the Oduduwa dynasty appropriated to itself after conquering Ile-Ife.[48]

The female Oduduwa's demise in the Ifa texts and in society is consistent with theories of how and in what stages of settlement males came to dominate society by disrupting women's close identification with the soil and its associated rituals. This seems to have been accomplished by adding a commercial role (marketwomanry) to women's aboriginal responsibilities as primary caregivers to their children and as horticulturists and producers of nutrients from the soil for the community. Men's increasing identification with agriculture, animal husbandry and the attendant rituals represented the shift in political authority[49] in Ile-Ife as in other primal societies.

A patriarchal policy and attitude has mediated the gendered society from the Oduduwa era to contemporary times. Though taken through training and an initiation akin to that of males, women are not fully initiated into the Ifa priesthood in Ile-Ife. They are initiated to be iyanifa and/or *apetibi*, i.e. for assistants to the babalawo tell me that Iyanifa therefore are given the opele chain but not ikin at the end of their Ifa initiation ritual; therefore, women Ifa diviners are known to use opele and cowry shells when they cast Ifa. Women also participate in Ifa rites through marriage to Ifa priests, so they become the female nurturers of Ifa—the go-fors, one might say for the babalawo. This state of affairs in Ifa is equivalent to gendered discrimination within the clergy of the Christian Church. Women in both faith traditions are protesting their marginalization.

Meanwhile, women of Ile-Ife assume roles that complement the work of the clergy. They are initiated as priestesses to other orishas, and many of the women diviners are initiated to Oshun, whose mythic being is owed to the era in which women seem to have originally devised and controlled divination. Women frequently also are mediums between the spirit realm and this world. These roles allow for a modicum of gendered complementarity, whereby family and society are maintained despite the negativity of the predominant patriarchy.[50] I cannot resist wondering how the gendered discrimination upsets the spiritual and social harmony that the Supreme Being sent divination to maintain.

Themes of transformation, continuity, and patriarchy are woven into the social fabric of Ile-Ife. From the above discussion, I find that the Yoruba are a mixed-race people, the divination canon is redacted to legitimize patriarchy and is called Odu Ifa, patriarchy displaced women's rights throughout society, and orisha worship and social values and mores are transformations engendered by political expediencies and temporal demands. It is against this historical and mythic backdrop of the Yoruba spiritual homeland that I discuss the founding and development of Oyotunji Village. By juxtaposing the two Yoruba communities—the former centuries-old and the latter a twentieth-century adaptation among Black Americans in the United States—we can acquire fresh insights into Yoruba traditional culture and the Ifa divination system.

Notes

1. Toyin Falola discusses conflation by chroniclers of the diverse groups of people into a collective Yoruba identity in *Yoruba Gurus: Indigenous Production of Knowledge in Africa* (Trenton: Africa World Press, Inc., 1999), Chapter 1.
2. Refer to *Olodumare: God in Yoruba Belief* (New York): Frederick A. Praeger, Publisher, 1963), 11.
3. Eluyemi, "The Role of Oral Tradition in the Archaeological Investigation of the History of Ife," in *Yoruba Oral Tradition*, ed. Wande Abimbola (Ile-Ife: University of Ife, 1975), 119-129 and Chief (Dr.) M.A. Fabunmi, *Ife: The Genesis of [the] Yoruba Race* (Ikeja, Lagos: John West Publications Ltd., 1985), 4.
4. A useful summary of the scientific histories and oral traditions is in Fabunmi, *Ife: The Genesis of [the] Yoruba Race*, 1-25 and refer to Oluyemi, "The Role of Oral Tradition in the Archaeological Investigation of the History of Ife" on the titles of kings at Ile-Ife.
5. Babatunde A. Agiri, "Yoruba Oral Tradition with Special Reference to the Early History of the Oyo Kingdom," in *Yoruba Oral Tradition*, ed. Wande Abimbola (Ile-Ife: University of Ife, 1975), 167-169. See a recent reference to Oduduwa as female deity in Dominique Zahan, "Some Reflections of African Spirituality," *African Spirituality: Forms, Meanings, and Expressions*, ed., Jacob K. Olupona (New York: Crossroad Publishing Company, 2000), 7. For more on Irunmoles, see Diedre Badejo, *Oshun: The Elegant Deity of Wealth, Power, and Femininity* (Trenton: Africa World Press, Inc., 73-85.
6. Fabunmi, *Ife: The Genesis of [the] Yoruba Race*, 22.
7. Adediran, *Frontier States of Western Yorubaland, 1600-1889* (Ibadan, Nigeria: French Institute for Research in Africa, 1994), 25-28, 55-59, and 68-71, where he refers to Samuel Johnson, History of the Yorubas (1921), 3-5 and Saburi O. Biobaku, The Origin of the Yoruba, (1955), 17-23; Fabunmi, *Ife: The Genesis of [the] Yoruba Race*, 22.
8. Agiri, "Yoruba Oral Tradition with Special Reference to the Early History of the Oyo Kingdom," 168.
9. Abimbola, *Sixteen Great Poems of Ifa* (UNESCO, 1975), 32, and Dr. Abosede Emanuel, *Odun Ifa* (Lagos, Nigeria: West African Book Publishers Limited, 2000), 79-95.

10. Excerpt from Abimbola, *Ifa: An Exposition of Ifa Literary Corpus* and in Fabunmi, *Ife: The Genesis of [the] Yoruba Race*, 214; on Christianity in Ile-Ife, refer to *IFE*, 96.
11. Wande Abimbola, *Sixteen Great Poems of Ifa*, 2-3.
12. Ibid, 4.
13. Ibid., 2, and Dr. Abosede Emanuel, *Odun Ifa*, 60-62.
14. Abimbola, *Sixteen Great Poems of Ifa*, 29-32.
15. Roland Abiodun, "Understanding Yoruba Art and Aesthetics: The Concept of Ashé," *African Arts* 27 (July 1994), 72.
16. Conrad E. Maugé, *The Yoruba World of Good and Evil* (Mount Vernon, N.Y.: House of Providence, 1994).
17. Abimbola, *Sixteen Great Poems of Ifa*, 8-32.
18. Ibid. For more information on the process of Ifa divination, refer to William Bascom, *Ifa Divination: Communication Between Gods and Men in West Africa* (Bloomington: Indiana University Press, 1969/1991) and the several other books on this subject in Chapter 1, n. 26.
19. Abimbola, *Sixteen Great Poems of Ifa*, 3. And John Henry Drewal, John Pemberton, II, and Roland Abiodun, *Yoruba: Nine Centuries of African Art and Thought* (New York: The Center for African Art in Association with Harry N. Abrams, Inc., 1989), 14.
20. Collected by author during field study in Ile-Ife in 1992; assisted in translations by Ile-Ife's chief Meyegun Adebayo Ogundijo.
21. Collected by author during his initiation into Ifa Priesthood, Conducted by Oyotunji African Village Chief Medahochi Omowale, in Gary, Indiana, 1979.
22. Refer to "Myth and Principle of Predestination in Yoruba Folk Culture," in *New York Folklore*, 10, nos. 1-2 (1984), 89, 90.
23. Abimbola, *Sixteen Great Poems of Ifa*, 39.
24. Ibid., 4; refer to Roland Abiodun, "Ifa Art Objects: An Interpretation Based on Oral Tradition," in *Yoruba Oral Tradition*, 424-425.
25. Abiodun, "Ifa Art Objects: An Interpretation based on Oral Tradition," 426, 458.
26. Abimbola, *Sixteen Great Poems of Ifa*, 9. In 1990 I observed Ile-Ife's Aseda Awo Adeyefa perform Ifa divination with

the opele. But, as I learned in later years in the Republic of Benin, divination can be accomplished with the use of two or three opeles. I witnessed the Fon (Fa) diviner Bokonon Kakanakou Gangbadji in 1998, 1999, and 2000 in Ouidah, employ two Ifa divining chains during Fa divinations. I have also observed Hounongan Agbegbe Guendehou Gbesso Baley in Cotonou, Benin Republic employ the use of three divining chains simultaneously.

27. Observation During Field Study in Ouidah and Cotonou, Republic of Benin. Summer, 2000.
28. *Sixteen Great Poems of Ifa*, 10.
29. *Journal of Culture and Ideas* 1, No. 1 (December 1983), 102, and Remy T. Hounwanou, *Le Fa: Une Geomancie Divinatoire du Golfe du Benin (pratique et technique)*, Les Nouvelles Editions Africaines, 1984, 24-25.
30. Bascom, *Ifa Divination*, 153.
31. *Journal of Culture and Ideas* 1, No. 1 (December 1983), 8-12.
32. Bascom, *Ifa Divination*, 94-95, with information paraphrased here.
33. This section on the religious order of the Awoni Chief Priests is based on the author's observations, Abimbola, *Sixteen Great Poems of Ifa*, 17 and Bascom, *Ifa Divination*, 94-95.
34. Ibid, 91-92, and based on conversations with Abimbola and members of the Awoni.
35. Ibid, 95.
36. Cheikh Anta Diop wrote about power and authority among African women in *Cultural Unity of Black Africa: The Domain of Patriarchy and of Matriarchy in Classical Antiquity* (Third World Press, 1990). Preferring not to call African matriarchs Amazons, he described the societies' appreciation for women and the prevalence of women rights, attributing it to their store of wisdom, in primal African societies. Valuing women for wisdom was operative in many ancient cultures. In the Old Testament Hebraic societies, Deborah and other women were valued for their inordinate wisdom. Consider that goddesses symbolized wisdom in Kamitic (ancient Egyptian); for Aset (orAst/Isis), refer to Jacob H. Carruthers, *Essay in Ancient Egyptian Studies* (Los Angeles: University of Sankore Press, 1984), 123. Hebrew

mythologies heralded feats of wise women— Aset/Ast (Isis), Sophia, and Hokmah. See Leonard Swidler's *Biblical Affirmations of Woman* (Philadelphia: Westminster Press, 1979), pp. 36-37 for blurbs on Sophia and Hokmah.

37. *Orunmila* (June 1990), No. 5, 10-11. The tradition of not allowing women to see Odu Ifa is tied to a set of taboos and prohibitions some of which are used to deny women of menstruating age, and also beyond, full rights to the Ifa Priesthood. Some scholars think the notion that women's mystical powers strengthen when they are menopausal period.

38. There are many works on African mythology; I only cite those that helped me to support this point. Among them are: Charles H. Long, *Alpha: The Myths of Creation* (New York: George Braziller, 1963), 9-28; Beier, ed., *Origin of Life and Death: African Creations Myths*; and Olatunde B. Lawuyi, "The Reality and Meaning of Being A Woman in the Yoruba Cosmogonic Myths: An Anthropologist's Contribution to O. Gbadegesin's 'Destiny, Personality and the Ultimate Reality and Meaning of Human Existence: A Yoruba Perspective,'" *Journal of Ultimate Meaning and Reality* 11, No. 3 (September, 1988); Badejo, *Oshun*, 73-74 & 91-92.

39. Adediran, *Frontier States of Western Yorubaland*, 68; Ulli Beier, "The History and Psychological Significance of Yoruba Myths," Odu 1 (1995), 20-21.

40. J.A. Atanda, "Origin of the Yoruba Reconsidered," *in Odu: A Journal of West African Studies*, New series, No. 25 (1984), 1-19, and refer to Lawuyi, "Reality and Meaning of Being a woman in the Yoruba Cosmogonic Myths," 233-242 and Bernard I. Belasco, *The Entrepreneur As Culture Hero: Preadaptations in Nigerian Economic Development* (New York: Praeger, 1980). Lillian Ashcraft-Eason writes about women's loss of social position in "Mythic Images of African Women in Marriage and Society Prior to the Transatlantic Slave Trade," *IFE: Annals of the Institute of Culture Studies*, No. 4 (Ile-Ife: Obafemi Awolowo University, 1993) for a bibliography and more discussion of transitions in women's roles in ancient societies.

41. Bascom, *Ifa Divination*, 82-83.

42. Consult "Gender Play," in *Yoruba Ritual* (Bloomington: Indiana University Press, 1992), 173.
43. Refer to *Orunmila* (June 1990), No. 5, 10-11 for Mrs. Ajanaku-Scott's statement.
44. *Abimbola, Sixteen Great Poems of Ifa*, 8.
45. *Ifa Divination*, 40 and Phillip M. Peek, ed., *African Divination Systems: Ways of Knowing* (Bloomington: University of Indians Press, 1991), 197.
46. *African Divination Systems*, 197.
47. *Frontier States of Western Yorubaland*, 42; Olupona, *Kingship, Religion and Rituals in A Nigerian Community: A Phenomenological Study of Ondo Yoruba Festivals* (Stockholm: Almquist & Wiksell International, 1991), 65-69.
48. Agiri, "Yoruba Oral Tradition with Special Reference to the Early History of the Oyo Kingdom," 169.
49. See on topic of shift in women's authority in primal societies Nancy Hafkin and Edna Bay, eds., *Women and Work in Africa: Studies in Social and Economic Change* (1976).
50. Niara Sudarkasa, "'The Status of Women' in Indigenous African Societies," in *Women in Africa and the African Diaspora*, ed., Rosalyn Terborg-Penn, Sharon Harley, and Andrea Benton Rushing (Washington, D.C.: Howard University Press, 1989); refer also to Margaret Thompson Drewal, "Gender Play," in *YORUBA RITUAL: Performers, Play, Agency* (Bloomington: Indiana University Press, 1992), 172-190.

Chapter 3
Oyotunji: African Americans Recover Ifa

Across the Atlantic Ocean, a small group of black-raced people—most of who never traveled to the Motherland—claimed descent from Africans enslaved in the Americas and began to call themselves Africans. It was a move inspired by independence in Ghana and Nigeria from British occupation and colonial rule as well as by the fervency of Black cultural nationalism in the United States. Black American participants in the politics of anticolonialism read about, and some had no doubt met, affable Yorubas. Most importantly, many lived among and observed black Cuban and Puerto Rican practitioners of Yoruba Traditional Religion. A clique of Black Americans determined that they would adopt Yoruba traditional culture and orisha worship for themselves. They also would call themselves Yorubas. The question that haunted the New Yorubas was: how could they authenticate themselves?

As an observer-participant who associated with the New Yoruba Movement before it became Oyotunji and who knew Oba Oseijeman and his first three initiates, I suggest an answer to the question that has lingered. An effective way to try to derive an answer is to treat Oyotunji immediately following my interpretative treatment of Ile-Ife. By juxtaposing the histories and development of two Yoruba communities—Ile-Ife and Oyotunji—the former centuries old and the latter a twentieth-century adaptation, I believe that fresh insights can be acquired into both and their celebration of Ifa.

A small group of African Americans banded together with Baba Oseijeman to establish the Oyotunji African Village in Sheldon, South Carolina in 1970. They installed Obatala, the orisha to whom Oseijeman was initiated in Matanzas, Cuba in 1959,[1] as the patron deity of the Village. Oseijeman was one of the first-known African Americans initiated into an African priesthood and introduced to divination and the Ifa canon in the twentieth century. Over the next forty-five years following his initiation, he pursued the vision of establishing African Traditional Religion in the United States.

This pursuit came at a time when most black Americans professed to be Christians and frowned on African religions, calling them pagan—if they acknowledged knowing anything at all about them. They certainly did not think that they could be accessed in the United States. During my childhood in the 1950s, only those religion scholars and dilettantes who studied African religions knew that Vodou had come to New Orleans at the turn of the nineteenth century with immigrants from Haiti. Resembling their African Traditional Religions, It thrived among the enslaved in the Catholic religious communities. In some places, the white political authorities of the localities permitted black nuns and priests to establish institutions that perhaps unknowingly sustained African Traditional religious practices. These religions were curiosities to most black and white folks. The religious experience was different in Protestant-dominated states where the parallels were less obvious and the African religious practices were castigated and banned by the slavocracy. In the Sea Islands off Georgia and South Carolina, descendants of enslaved Africans retained aspects of African Traditional Religions but claimed no knowledge of how the remnants related to African religious systems.

By the late fifties, folks interested in reclaiming the sacred religious traditions of their West African ancestors had to search outside the United States. Some went to Africa in their search and others to Caribbean and South American countries. They had heard about African spirituality and practices in those places largely from Latinos who immigrated to urban centers—primarily to New York City—in the United States. Latinos boasted to their African-American acquaintances that a viable West African religious heritage had been retained in Cuba, Brazil, Puerto Rico, Haiti, Trinidad, and other Afro-Latin areas of the Americas. An occasional African American lamented that the religions of their African ancestors were lost to Blacks in North America, and they determined to learn about them.

Oseijeman, who was named Walter Eugene King at his birth on October 5, 1928 in Detroit, wanted to know Africa and African religions. Details of his family life during his formative years, as laid out in studies by Carl Hunt and Tracey Hucks, indicate that an African identity prevailed. In elementary school, King wondered why African Americans had no religious holidays with which to identify as a community as the Jews in school with him had. Reared in a black

Baptist church, he and his older brother expressed concern that their church lacked an African identity. He stopped attending the church during his early teens, declaring that it had neither an African God nor African orientation.

As a student at Cass Technical High School, Walter's African consciousness was further awakened by his association with fellow student Crandall Eaton. The boys read articles on African cultures and religions in *National Geographic*, learned of ethnic differences, and took African names. Walter's curiosity about the African ancestral heritage continued through his introduction to African Dance by Leroi Jones (now Amiri Baraka), who directed the local Pen and Palette Club. This infatuation with Africa continued through King's travels in Chicago, Los Angeles, and subsequently in Paris with the Katherine Dunham dancers. His focus on Africa decreased when Dunham sent him from Paris to New York to learn her dance technique.

The curiosity that impelled him to study African dances and cultures also motivated him to pursue life in general with vigor. Entering what Hucks called his European period, he married Jan, a woman of Dutch ancestry in 1951 and delved into ballet and other Euro-centric art. He assumed several cultural identities and immersed himself in art, dance, theater, and small business enterprise.[2] Aware of his wife's cultural identity, he sensed that he could not fully internalize the European arts and culture. He felt alienated and began reading about Africa, attending black theater, engaging in creative writing on black topics, and assuming membership in sundry black organizations. Although he took time to learn about religions from black Haitian and Cuban immigrants to New York City, he had no African intimates and learned about

African religions and culture from books during lengthy bouts at the Schomburg.

In interviews that he granted in later life, he recalled his childhood exposure to Egyptian religion through the cartoons of J.A. Rodgers in the *Pittsburgh Courier* and said that he had read George Washington Williams' *History of the Negro Race, 1619-1880* (1883). King was deeply impressed by Mbonu Ojike's *My Africa* (1946), particularly in his charges that Christianity and Islam had disrupted African lifestyles. From Ojike, he also learned that there were many African religions and African gods. Ojike's book reminded King that he and Eaton had read about diverse African cultures in *National Geographic* during their youth.[3] The readings, local black cultural arts performances and exhibits, conversations with black immigrants from the Caribbean, and discussions during meetings of organizations that he joined whetted King's appetite to learn more about Africa and the Diaspora.

King began to travel and study specific religious systems. With his wife, he visited Egypt, Haiti, and Cuba in 1956. Along the way, he assumed the name Oseijeman (Akan meaning "savior of the people"). Upon his return from Haiti, he founded the Dahomean-Haitian Order of *Dambada Hwedo*. This order revered the Dahomean deity Dambada, who symbolized the collective, honored, ancient ancestors. It would be the first of several Afrocentric organizations that Oseijeman founded and touted to establish his affinity for African religions. When *Dahomey: An Ancient West African Kingdom* (in 2 volumes) by Melville J. Herskovits was published in 1957, Oseijeman read it to increase his knowledge of Dambada Hwedo and to enhance his practice in the priesthood based on what he observed in Haiti and New York.

Chapter 3

When the 29-year-old Oseijeman learned about Ghanaian culture from the publicity of that country's independence celebration in 1957, he added the title *Nana* (chief in Akan) to his Akan name and moved the Dambada Hwedo Order to 125th Street in Harlem. There his close associate was Haitian singer and actor Fritz Vincent, who was knowledgeable about the religion. Guided by images from books and memories of the religion from his travels in Haiti, Nana Oseijeman used skills from his studies at Cass Technical High School and the Pen and Palette Art Club in Detroit to build shrines, altars and statues of the Vodoun.

He left the Order of Dambada Hwedo in 1959 after its members seemed more interested in philosophizing about African religions than in reclaiming them as lived-experience. Some temple members argued that African Americans would not be persuaded to accept African Traditional Religions and pantheons of deities. Oseijeman articulated his interest in African religions and in proselytizing them among African Americans.

Soon after withdrawing from the order, Nana Oseijeman met Christopher Oliana, a black Cuban practitioner of Santeria in New York. Oseijeman's interest in their conversations about Santeria, stemmed from his belief that it was a continuation of a West African tradition. He soon became aware of Santeria's Catholic elements and use of European-complexioned and -styled Catholic saints. In a divination for Oseijeman, Oliana advised him to purchase and place in his restaurant a statue of Sainte Barbara, whom Oliana had determined to be Oseijeman's guardian protector. Repulsed by the thought of praying to a white saint, the black nationalist-minded Oseijeman refused Oliana's advise but did inquire as to whether he could become an African priest. Receiving an affirmative response, Oseijeman traveled with Oliana to Matanzas for initiation during the period of relative calm that preceded the outbreak of the Cuban revolution in 1959.

After returning from Cuba, he organized the Shango Temple at East 125th Street and incorporated into it influences from Dahomean and Haitian religious traditions. He installed Shango, intending this icon to be an African deity, in the temple and began to use the Yoruba-priestly title Baba. He now realized that Cubans had altered African traditions radically, intermingling them with Catholic rituals and theology and deriving the culturally eclectic Santeria. He read about Yoruba Traditional Religion in the Reverend Olumide Lucas' book, *The Religion of the Yoruba* (1948). He began to talk about purifying Santeria for African Americans.

For Oseijeman, purifying Santeria meant taking out what was not African. He surrounded himself with like-minded people. In 1960, he changed the name of Shango Temple to Yoruba Temple, moving it to West 116th Street, and he pruned away what he thought to be vestiges of Santeria. It was a rule that no one could enter the temple unless dressed in African attire. Assemblies at the temple consisted mainly of *bembes* (ceremonies in which Yoruba orisha worshippers beat out drum rhythms, danced, and chanted), teachings on Yoruba religion, and offerings to the Yoruba deities.

Oseijeman set up the African Theological Archministry as an institution incorporated under the state of New York as an adjunct to the temple. The Archministry published and disseminated information about Yoruba Traditional Religion and orishas. The archministry ordained priests, performed ceremonies, chanted, preached, divined, and danced to the deities (orishas) of the Yoruba. This latter move and Oseijeman's adoption of the title Baba symbolized his split with the Cubans whose interests were in Santeria and Cuban nationalism, not in reclaiming and revitalizing the religions of Africa.

Looking back in the late sixties over his life as a teenager, Oseijeman traced his growing interest in Africa. He recalled that during the 1940s he had began to feel that his destiny was to awaken his African identity. He told the chronicler of Oyotunji's history, Carl Hunt, that

> By the time he was fifteen he was secretly questioning the relevance of Western religion to Black people. By the time he was sixteen, he was openly questioning Christianity.... "By ... seventeen years old, ... [he] was out of the Church completely." The element that erased any doubts about the validity of Christianity and the Black experience was his reading of Mbonu Ojike's *My Africa*.[4]

Oseijeman asserted that his parents had taught him to be concerned about the condition of black people in the United States. His father implanted the idea that African Americans would find freedom by identifying with Africa in him. Those recollected admonitions combined in Oseijeman's mind in a way that made him want to free African Americans by exhorting them to embrace African religions. During the Sixties, Malcolm X, Baraka, and Karenga exhorted Americans to free themselves by adopting African cultures. Religion and black cultural nationalism were the duality that drove him toward his mission of calling black people to adopt African cultures.

Oseijeman believed that a nationalistic and spiritual ethos persisted but lay dormant among Black Americans, and he wanted to awaken it. He wondered how the political and religious dynamics could be harnessed to the best advantage of African Americans. In his mind, Black Nationalism ultimately should take on the characteristics of an African state with African Traditional Religion as its foundation.

During a 1962 rally of the African National Independence Party founded by him in New York, he announced that by 1972, an African state—identifiable by its practice of African religious traditions—would exist in the United States. He encouraged members of the party to wear African clothes to begin to prepare for that eventuality. He, too, prepared by divorcing Jan in 1963 and adopting the Yoruba traditional practice of polygamy. He took several black women as wives, including Asunta Serrano (An Afro-Puerto Rican, Santerian priestess). He instituted an annual Africa Day Parade that brought him celebrity in New York and other parts of the United States. Oseijeman thought he detected an escalating interest in African religions among Black Americans. He begun to entertain the thought that Black Americans might eventually be awakened and that an African settlement inside the United States might be a result of the enthusiasm that he perceived.

Black Americans from many parts of the United States tried to contact Oseijeman as the work of the party and its African religious ethos spread. They came to the temple from various parts of the East Coast, requesting advice on sundry problems and asking for African names. In 1960 *Hep* magazine published an interview with Oseijeman, dubbing him "Voodoo Priest in Harlem." The article included a photograph of a keen-featured, light-complexioned man, who by his looks could claim a number of nationalities, but he was claiming to be African.

Most people did not know what to make of him and the religion that he practiced in the Temple and in his apartment, to which Christians and Muslims went with their problems. Because of his associations with Malcolm X's rallies, some thought the Yoruba Temple was Muslim. Because he said that he was practicing Yoruba Traditional Religion when making tribute to the orishas, addressing the problems of clients by divining, offering sacrifices, and practicing polygamy, many thought Oseijeman was pagan and heathen, if not immoral. Not even the writer of the *Hep* article had known enough to distinguish among African Traditional Religions or to understand how Oseijeman was deriving as much as he could about them from informants, books, and his own observations of Santeria and Haitian Vodou.

The *Hep* article inspired James Butler (then known as Omowale—an employee of U.S. Steel—who later took the Fon title, Medahochi, for teacher by which he is widely known today) and some of his associates to open a Yoruba Temple in Gary, Indiana in 1962. This was two years after he had begun his search to locate Baba Oseijeman in order to learn more about his movement and perhaps join him.[5] Four years after reading the *Hep* article, Omowale and two cohorts actually saw Oseijeman. That meeting would be one road leading to the later establishment of Oyotunji, for Omowale's vision and persistence in pursuing a Black-American revivified, African religion would be pivotal.

As Omowale recalled in 1991 and 1992 taped interviews with me (by which time he was known as Medahochi—the name that I will use hereafter), three men from Gary made the trip to New York

City to meet Baba Oseijeman. They found him after going to the bookstore owned by Lonnie Michaux, proprietor of the National Memorial Bookstore in Harlem. Recalling this search Medahochi said, "When we inquired about Baba Oseijeman, Michaux told us immediately about this man. Michaux said, 'Come back at 2:00, and you'll see the woman who works for him.'" Her name was Mama Keke, an immigrant from Barbados. She was a member of the Yoruba Temple in New York City and had been since 1960.[6] Medahochi contacted her, and she gave him Baba Oseijeman's telephone number. The Gary group and Baba Oseijeman eventually met. After the Gary group returned home, their communication with Oseijeman continued.

Baba Oseijeman and Mama Keke went to the Yoruba Temple in Gary in March 1964 and officiated over seven *eleke* ceremonies. Seven people, that is, received five necklace-length strands of sacred beads representing the colors and numbers of five Orishas. Some of the Gary group also received the image of Elegba. Others received, in addition, a container called an Ogun pot that held iron instruments, significant armor for warriors striving to establish a Black American-centered African Traditional Religion in the United States. In all three instances, the decision as to who should receive which orisha symbols was determined by the person's perceived spirituality as indicated by Merindinlogun divinations. After that visit, the Gary group sent for Baba Oseijeman a number of times, and Yoruba Traditional Religion and divination had presence in the Mid-West from that time.[7]

At the end of the decade, concern about the direction that the Temple should take and pressures from Cubans opposed to the Africanization of Santeria convinced Oseijeman that it was time for him to leave New York. With others in the Temple, he came to believe that African Americans needed to pursue a destiny that was in conflict with interests of Cuban immigrants and white Americans. No longer as separatist in his thinking as the Republic of New Africa had been during its conference in 1968, Oseijeman reasoned that members of the Yoruba Temple should not leave the United States but should live apart from the general society. They should show that they could stay and survive. Moreover, he thought they did not need to take the Yoruba Religion to Africa, where it already was. They needed to proselytize it among black Americans as a tool for helping themselves transcend their economic and social plight.

These men of hope recognized that they themselves needed economic autonomy, because their dependence on jobs would not allow them freedom to practice an "African [traditional] lifestyle on a daily basis."[8] They began to inquire about purchasing land in the rural South, a space more suitable than the New York metropolis for rehabilitating the African American psyche.

The governing society of the Yoruba Temple—the *Ogboni* (This was a group that began as a men's secret organization in Ile-Ife in opposition to the Oduduwa regime. In Oyotunji, it was the men's council that set policy.)—determined through divination that Oseijeman should accept a job offer to teach African history in Transitional Academy, a pre-college preparatory school for black children in Bricks, North Carolina. He went to the South in July 1969. After the academy closed in September, Oseijeman settled on moving into a house of antebellum-vintage in Savannah, Georgia.

Still thinking entrepreneurially, his intention was to open an African coffee shop. Following a number of financial difficulties associated with having several wives (not a helpful, established lifestyle in the United States as it was in agrarian-based Africa) and a growing family, in a city, in an old house needing constant repairs, he looked to relocate in 1970. Penniless, he encircled himself with drawings of astrological and orisha figures. Standing in the middle, Oseijeman called on the orishas for help. Today he believes that they directed him to ask two friends in New York (Akinyele Awolowo and Kofi Aderemi Omowale) to send him money. He took the $250.00, rented a U-Haul truck, drove with his family to South Carolina, and people there told him about a house for lease outside Beaufort on Paige's Point Road. This move to a house in a rural area was fortuitous. The trudge toward building an African settlement accelerated.

After Oseijeman moved to South Carolina, three people—Akinyele Awolowo who had been with him in New York since 1966, Akanke of Gary, and Medahochi went to South Carolina in 1970 for initiations.[9] Medahochi was the catalyst for this step. He had been contending for several months with Baba Oseijeman that he should begin to initiate priests into the Yoruba Temple. During a visit to Paige's Point, Awolowo joined Medahochi in making the case. The two men argued that the Cubans could have initiated them. But, they reasoned that if they had to depend on non-African Americans to initiate them into African religions, the religion would be foreign-influenced. So they insisted that Oseijeman, who had not initiated anyone by himself and was not at that time a babalawo, initiate them.

Oseijeman, who had learned rituals of initiation from Santeras, consulted Ifa through Merindinlogun. Confident that the readings signaled him to proceed, he conducted a series of initiations, with the assistance of one of his wives—Olubunmi Omi Tonade. Olubunmi had learned the role of apetebi from Assunta and other Santeria women while at the Yoruba Temple. She knew how to support priests in initiation rituals and now began to assist Baba Oseijeman. A Nigerian priest, whose name is remembered as Ojo, subsequently taught him more about Yoruba religion and about Ogun rituals in particular.[10]

Awolowo was first in the line of Oseijeman's initiates because, in accordance with Yoruba religious protocol, he was to be initiated to Obatala who always takes precedence. Upon his initiation, Awolowo became Elemosha and soon thereafter, Oseijeman bestowed the chieftaincy upon him. Akanke's initiation to *Yemoja* followed the next day, and her priestly name became Omilade. Later that same day Medahochi's initiation to Shango proceeded, and he became Shangodele.[11] Three more initiations were held there in August 1970. Those six initiations, conducted at Baba Oseijeman's home on Paige's Point Road in April 1970, began the Yoruba-derived, African-American orisha controlled, priesthood in North America.

As the movement strengthened and its work with the priestly order increased, there was need for more land for building a settlement. Robert and Belle Smalls, an African American couple, rented an old farmhouse and land on their Brays Island Road property to Oseijeman in late 1970. From December 1970 through October 1972, there were fourteen initiations at Brays Island Road. The first initiation at the present Oyotunji site was performed in the fall of 1972. (See listing of these initiations in Appendix).[12] With the establishment of a self-perpetuating priesthood, the African American Yoruba community had actually established the Yoruba Traditional Religion.

Elemosha, Omilade, and Shangodele (Medahochi) returned to their respective homes in New York and Gary after their initiations. The first permanent resident on Bray's Island Road with Baba Oseijeman and his wives was Kpojito Hwesihuno, who was initiated in August 1970; after going back to Gary, she returned to live on Brays Island Road in November. She remained there until November 1972. Only Elemosha of the first three initiates returned to live in community with Baba Oseijeman and his wives for several years. Some initiates remained in the Village in Sheldon after their initiations; one of these was Chief Eleshin, who lived in Oyotunji Village. Two priests (Chief Akintobe and Chief Olofundeyi Olaitan—seen in the videoclip in the role of Alaagba) who were initiated in Oyotunji in 1977 and 1978 respectively continue to live there. Chief Edubi Ajamu, initiated in October 1972, has not lived there continuously but frequently was in residence over extended periods.

Most of the initiates into the movement never lived in Oyotunji; they scattered around the country and established their own temples with their own improvisations on the Yoruba religious traditions. Priests/esses are obligated to return to the Village a few months after completing their initiations to have their orishas and their divining implements reinvigorated.

In his rapport with the scattered priests, Oseijeman adopted the kingship model described by Samuel Johnson. Writing from the perspective of the Oyo kingdom, Johnson stated that the alafin (king of Oyo) was paramount over the other Yoruba kings, but this view is generally discredited today. There were many independent kingdoms among the people that we now know as Yoruba. Nevertheless, before the nineteenth century, Oyo was the largest and most powerful Yoruba kingdom, inclining Oseijeman and followers to name their village after that kingdom. The relationship between Oseijeman and his initiates is a religious rather than political one. In Yoruba religion, the godfather of an initiate maintains a tributary allegiance with the godfather. Building on this allegiance, the Oba has established a system of chiefs who are in Oyotunji and scattered around the country. A culture of allegiance-to-religion and founder is the glue that supports this system, for Oseijeman has no legal authority for enforcing it.

At the Brays Island site the first sign announcing the "Yoruba African Cultural Center" was hung in 1971. This marked the official birth of the African village. Oseijeman explained that after leaving Brays Island Road, he and his followers chose the name Oyotunji "which means 'Oyo rises again,' because Oyo was one of the empires created by the Yoruba peoples."[13] They transferred the sign to the present site and added, "You are leaving the United States of America and entering Africa." They intended that the sign would prepare people for the rustic nature of the Village while heightening their anticipation. People, such as Ojo, who were from Nigerian towns could see how closely Oyotunji replicated a Yoruba traditional village in architectural design and life-style. Although he had visited Oyo and Ile-Ife, Oseijeman primarily had researched in books to get his design.

Run-ins with the law, negative talk about the Yoruba-derived life-style, and ceremonial rituals with animal sacrifices raised eyebrows among the locals. Partially adorned bodies, animal sacrifices and polygamy (that was banned for anyone who came to the village after 1974), particularly disturbed area residents. The proprietor evicted the Oyotunji villagers from Brays Island Road in 1972. After acquiring ten acres of land with a house nearby and still along Route 21, Oyotunji villagers set about the three- to four-month task of moving the settlement to the new site. They cleared forests, laid out a road, and began to construct new buildings. It was just prior to the move from Bray's Island Road to the present location that I began to frequent the Village (as stated in Chapter 1). I used my "ancient" Volkswagen bus to assist Chief Elemosha with the moving. It is my memory that he had charge of the Village and of completing the relocation while Oseijeman was in Abeokuta, Nigeria receiving his initiation into the Ifa Priesthood.

Despite the burden of relocating the Village, Baba Oseijeman had found irresistible the unexpected opportunity to travel to West Africa. The dance troupe of Dinizulu of New York City invited him, who had been the troupe's announcer before moving South, to accompany them on an all-expenses-paid trip to Ghana. Oseijeman thought this was fortuitous because prior to his break with the Cubans, he had received a divination advising that he was to become a babalawo. He realized that the trip could provide him an opportunity to travel from Ghana to Nigeria for possible initiation. He traveled to Abeokuta, Nigeria and was initiated to Ifa.[14]

Soon after moving to the present site in 1972, residents in the Village coronated him king of Oyotunji, and he began to use the title, Oba (king) Oseijeman. He is Chief Priest and chief administrator of the Village although the Ogboni (governing council) advises him on matters of policy and communal planning. Like their African counterparts who are devotees of divination, the Ifa oracle is the final arbiter of all matters. In 1981, Ooni Sijuwade and the chiefs of Ile-Ife installed Oseijeman as a balé (village head), strengthening Oseijeman's relationship with the kingdom and his stature as king to Oyotunji loyalists.

Religion was the most significant organizing principle for ancient Yoruba societies. Modeled after them as nearly as possible within modern America, life in Oyotunji has not had a sacred-secular dichotomy. The Yoruba sacred worldview informs everyday thinking and calibrates behavior. Ifa divination, with either *ikin* or *opele* chain as the occasion dictates, occurs regularly in order to detect the wishes of the orishas for the lives of the people there. Life is controlled by the orishas, for "they believe in the will of the deities, ... [who] control their lives from birth to death and even into the after life."[15]

When considering their move to the present site, the villagers realized that they needed enough land to have room for altars and shrines to the several orishas that they worship. These include Obatala (creation and executive functions), Elegba/Eshu (messenger of the orishas and so inseparable from Ifa/Orunmila), Ogun (iron and war), Ochosi (forest and vegetation), Shango (thunder and justice), Oshun (creative arts and fertility), Yemoja (river and nurturing), Olokun (sea), Egungun/Dambada Hwedo (ancestors), Ibeji (twins), and Ifa (divination oracle). There are priests and temples devoted to the worship of Obatala, Oshun, Ogun, Shango, Ifa, Olokun, and Dambada Hwedo, and Yemoja, and there are priests devoted to Yemoja and Elegba.

All adults in Oyotunji pay homage to several orishas. Because Oseijeman was initiated to Obatala and this orisha is the Village's patron deity, everyone who lives there must participate in worship of him. All adults have pots symbolically containing spirits of their family members in the Dambada Hwedo Temple, where they worship that Vodoun. Because of the centrality of Ifa divination in Yoruba Traditional Religion, everybody pays homage to this orisha.

Some priests have supported Oyotunji while pursuing their own experimentation with African religions outside the village. In the early 1970s Shangodele, for example, mixed the Yoruba with Dahomean traditions, after he had assumed the Fon title, *Medahochi* (elder). This followed from his associations in Atlanta with the Kpojito (Omiyeye Hwesihuno), who had left Oyotunji in November 1972. Oseijeman experimented almost from the beginning, mixing Yoruba and Fon names. He added Adefunmi (a Yoruba name meaning "crown given to me,") to his Akan names and gave Mrs. Ademuyinwa (Kpojito) the Yoruba name Omiyeye and a Fon name (Hwesihuno) at her initiation in 1970. She moved to Atlanta and expanded her passion for the orishas to include more Vodou. Only after settling in Atlanta did Kpojito assume this Fon title (meaning wife of the leopard, a totem of the Fon). Kpojito, Medahochi, and Omilade (who added the Fon title Toyevi (daughter) to her name) began to systematically incorporate Dahomean elements into the practice of Yoruba religion.

Following the death and entombment at Oyotunji of Chief Elemosha in 1990, the most senior priest after Oseijeman in the Oyotunji movement is Medahochi. As mentioned above, he is significant as an innovating force within the movement. Named James Butler at birth in 1923 in Rutherford County, Tennessee, he exhibited intellectual and artistic abilities early in life and began studying African history and culture in the 1940s. He attended Tennessee State University in Nashville and served in the war before going to work in the U.S. Steel plant in Gary, where he retired in the mid-eighties.[16] Currently residing in Milwaukee, he

Chapter 3

is a Chief Priest of Ifa in the Oyotunji Royal African Archministry and an official representative of Oba Oseijeman. He also is a revered elder and teacher in and beyond Oyotunji circles. Medahochi discussed the eclecticism indicative of innovation within the Oyotunji Movement, mentioning the Fon names that he gave to two initiates in 1978—Jesse Johnson from Albany, Georgia, who became Tosu Tosasalem (in the spirit of *Naete*, the sea goddess) and me—Adelade—Djisovi (Adjakta/Hevioso), the eighth and ninth initiates in Medahochi's temple in Gary.

Medahochi continued in the Dahomean tradition when he initiated several of us as Fa Priests in 1979, intending to add an indigenized dimension to initiation ceremonies. In this experiment, he used neither *iyerosun* nor *ikin* but did derive our Fa Du (*Woli Fun*) by divining with acorns that he had specially prepared. I was one of about eight males whom he took through a *Fazume* (forest) experience. He deciphered the Fa Du by etching the characters in the soil rather than in *iyerosun* on a divining tray. At the end of the ceremony, Medahochi scooped up the soil in which he had etched the Fa Du and handed it to each of the neophytes. Thus, Medahochi experimented with indigenizing the ritual, using soil and acorns to initiate us as Ifa diviners. Subsequently, I received an *opele* from Medahochi so that I had tools of the Ifa/Fa diviner and could practice the skills. In 1987 Oba Oseijeman carried me through an Ifa initiation ceremony and presented me with Odu Ifa and a "hand of Ifa" (eight *ikin*), completing my initiation to Ifa. The innovative potential of the Oyotunji Movement was impressive to me.

Not only did Medahochi experiment with indigenizing initiation ceremonies, but he stated in 1992 that he and Oba Oseijeman intended to pan-Africanize the religion. He expounded on this point:

> The difference between your initiations and the ... [previous ones] was that we began to include in that 1978 initiation orisha-vodun [joint Yoruba-Dahomean rituals] whereas earlier initiations were . . . [intentionally] orisha. But as you know the system that was devised by Oba Oseijeman is actually Yoruba-orisha and Fon-vodun. That means that we recognize ... the vodun along with the orisha. Since 1978, Oba Oseijeman and I have begun to include the *nkisi* from the Congo as well as the vodun and orisha. The orisha-vodun[-nkisi] is a pan-African ritualistic system with all of the authentic African entities equally incorporated or equally accepted. So there is no need for us to have a distinct ... system [of] vodoun .., orisha ... [, and nkisi] when we [can have a pan-African] religious tradition.[17]

This experimentation was owed to the thinking that Black Americans did not know if they had Yoruba, or Kongolese, or Dahomean (Fon) ancestry or not. Therefore, they did not obligate themselves to practice any one tradition, although they had declared themselves to be New Yorubas. He thought Black Americans should be pan-African in their adoption of African Traditional religions and cultures.

The Oyotunji Movement's appropriation of African religious traditions, therefore, is uneven. The number of initiates to nkisi is negligible, possibly because religion in Oyotunji centers on orisha-vodun. Among the eclectic aspects of Yoruba Traditional Religion in the Oyotunji Movement are lingering influences from Santeria. The Cuban influence is observable in the display of glasses of water, candles, cigars, and photos that clients are advised to place on ancestral altars, as well as in the wearing of elekes that represent the seven major orishas/vodouns. Oseijeman's friend, Dinizulu, adopted Akan culture and religion (Akom) in Jamaica, Queens, New York from about 1971; but he also taught and exhibited performing arts of diverse African peoples. Acknowledging the need for innovation, Oba Oseijeman "advocated that the (re)creation and (re)invention of traditional African religion was a required element in the restoration and reconstruction of the battered African American image and identity."[18] They were willing to claim identification with a single African tradition while being eclectic in ritualistic and artistic practices.

Indigenization and pan-Africanization dilute tendencies toward tribalism in Oyotunji. These features are more consistent with the African American identity that does not know specific ancestral origins. The improvisations are intended to unify the African Americans who are priests/esses to deities in different African Traditional Religions.

Oyotunji seeks to extend its influence beyond both its initiates and the geographical parameters of the Village. Theoretically it encompasses all African Americans for purposes of proselytizing. It is the collective body of Oba Oseijeman and all who have been initiated in Oyotunji Village, the initiates of those priests/esses, and those who followed in those lines. Oyotunji is referred to as a movement because its adherents have the specific, concerted goal of reclaiming and uniting African Americans in a pan-Africanized version of Yoruba religion and away from a Euro-centric, Christian psyche.[19]

The importance of Ifa in Oyotunji was symbolized in the moribund journal, *IFA*, with the Oba as Editor-in-Chief and Medahochi as its Managing Editor. The cover of the journal identified Ifa as "the light, guide, counselor, and friend of our forefather." A verse from *Odu Otura-Ka*, printed in Yoruba and English, described the possibilities of Ifa for redeeming people:

> Orunmila said, "Osuuru-suuru;"
> I responded, "Osuuru-suuru."
> He asked, "Who is there behind washing head?"
> We replied, "But it is you Orunmila!"
> He made his lamentation a lamentation of shout;
> He made his voice the voice of (Ifa) song.
> He sang—
> "Head washed by adept, is washed for longevity;
> Head washed by adept, is washed for haleness;
> Head washed by adept, is washed for purity."

This verse reminding readers that Ifa cleanses the skillful and knowledgeable for positive endeavors ends with the greeting for babalawos: "Aboru Aboye."

During the 1990s, Medahochi arranged a worship order that he called Ijo Orunmila Amerika. One aspect of the order of worship consisted of "Praises and Greetings to the Holy Spirit of Destiny (*Oriki Orunmila Mimo*)." This worship concept and the journal displayed some of the creative reaches of the Oba and Medahochi as they attempted to make literature and activities of the Yoruba Traditional Religion and Ifa accessible to African Americans.

Oyotunji has sought to encourage African Americans to link with Africa as homeland of Black peoples. Knowing that he had searched for meaning in other religions before settling on the Yoruba religion, I asked Medahochi why he had not become Buddhist or Muslim or Christian. Because, he said, those religions did not speak to the African American desire for an African ancestral identity enough to inspire commitment. He believed, moreover, that he was inspired to pursue African Traditional Religions by his ancestors. He recalled that during his youth in the 1930s and 1940s, there seemed to be no books about either Africa or languages and traditions available to him in either educational or religious institutions, so he surmised that Africa must be in his DNA.

In spite of that unfortunate situation as a child, he felt that there had to be a link between himself and the African continent. He recalled that the first African word he ever heard was "Nyumum [good]." "My mother," he recalled, "always used this word and the word 'goober' [peanut]. These were the only African words I remember encountering as a youth, and they had to hold me until I could find more ... later in my adult life."[20] Thus, Medahochi reminded me that although Africa may lie dormant in the hearts and minds of many African Americans, some recall a word, an aphorism, a song, a tale, a superstition handed down from African forebears and heard at the knees of older family members.

Ancestors are important to the Yoruba. Honoring them takes on an air of urgency with African-conscious black Americans, because they know that they connect them to the continent. Every time Oyotunji villagers say morning prayers, they honor their ancestors whose names they no longer remember, both those in Africa and those enslaved in America. They hasten to make a roll call of those maternal and paternal ancestors whose names they remember. Virtually every person for whom Oseijeman has cast

Ifa is reminded to revere the ancestors, and Oyotunji has been performing elaborate rituals honoring them since the early 1970s, as I noted in my references to the egungun society.

Egungun ceremonies that Oyotunji perform honor the composite ancestors of the African Americans, ancestors of the oba and his family, ancestors of other villagers. This ritual is derived from the Nigerian Yoruba who have memorialized egungun rituals in the Ifa canon. Egungun rituals are masquerades representing an ancestral spirit visiting its former community. In its appearance, the egungun is wrapped in voluminous, often multi-colored garments.[21] The Yoruba refer to egunguns as *"ara orun,"* beings from the spirit world of deceased ancestors.[22] The preparations and ceremonies require religious specialists, headed by an official called alaagba, who undertake "funerary rites, commemorative rites for the deceased, and masked performances designed for public festivals."[23] The style and time of appearance of an egungun masquerade ultimately is partially determined by an Ifa divination although cost and availability of specialized priests also are among factors determining scheduling.

Egungun masks are among the Yoruba's most elaborate visual and performance art forms. It is no wonder that they are presented at Oyotunji, where art is used ritualistically and to capture attention of the public long enough to teach and invite inquiry about the Yoruba religion and about African religions and cultures generally. There is other artistic performance at Oyotunji. Oba Oseijeman is accomplished in the dances of the orisha and the cult of Ifa, and he is an enchanting vocal artist. For hours, he can mesmerize listeners with narrations and interpretations of myths and his own odyssey as an Oyotunji-Yoruba leader.

It is no exaggeration to say that visual artists and craftspersons have played significant roles in the Oyotunji-Yoruba religious movement. One of the most inspired, productive and imaginative of these is Oba Oseijeman.[24] True to the folk-artist prototype, he uses his artistic gifts to articulate who the Yoruba and other Africans were in antiquity and in traditional times/places and what the enslaved Africans became as a result of how racism and politics in the United States impacted them. His work derives primarily from the desire to decorate the ritualistic vessels, altars, temples, and buildings of the Oyotunji African Village. For him art has utility in religious ritual, ceremony, and architecture.

Oba Oseijeman saw "art as an instrument . . . [for] revolutionary change."[25] No artist within the Oyotunji movement has used her/his artistic skills toward trying to foment change in the psyches of black Americans more than he. Oseijeman, with men like Chief Elemosha, built and decorated many of the buildings at Oyotunji. A significant number of religious sculptings stand along side buildings, jut out of eaves, and/or stand in fields between buildings, at the edges of surrounding woods, and in meeting rooms and temples. A brief tour of these premises allows one to observe the array of sculpted and painted images of Yoruba, Fon, and Egyptian deities.[26] They are useful as sacred theatrical sets for religious ritualistic performances and festivals. Based on archival research and field studies it is my assessment that Oyotunji African Village adheres to the basic Yoruba traditional Ile-Ife architecture with some decorative variations, like the Egyptian and ancient Dahomean mythic themes in paintings in particular.

Oyotunji has brought innovations to the images and symbols of the orisha and vodun. These innovations are displayed in Oseijeman's *oshe Shango* carvings and Elemosha's image of Shango, which Robert Farris Thompson describes in *Flash of the Spirit*.[27] Chief Medahochi added to this legacy with the decorated gourds that he presented to priests/esses whom he initiated. Upon my initiation to Adjakata/Hevioso, Medahochi presented that vodoun's implements to me in a large, colorfully painted gourd. Its attractiveness is easily recognizable as visual art.[28] Medahochi's paintings illustrate and interpret Odu Ifa/Fa Du, orisha-vodouns, and other aspects of Yoruba Traditional Religion.

Medahochi's attire and philosophical demeanor appeal to the curious, particularly when they hear that he is the creator of the art. Wearing his hair shaved except for a small braided plait at the back and dressed in a white tunic-styled outfit with pants and a cap, he obviously is not standard Black American. This difference in attire might attract people to him to ask about his visual art. His story telling skills give him opportunity to proselytize Yoruba and Fon Religions to the curious inquire.[29]

Oyotunji has the burden of trying to publicize among and familiarize the African American community with Yoruba Traditional Religion so that they can share what the devotees believe is beneficial. Most African Americans don't know that Oyotunji exists, so the Village has to proselytize its salvific aims and herald its existence. Villagers accept invitations to speak and perform in schools and universities, on local community programs, and in churches, and they announce their respective locations, audiovisual and print materials, consultative services, and celebrative activities on the Internet. An appearance on the Oprah Winfrey Show and occasional newspaper and magazine articles have given the Village entree to the sphere of popular culture.

There is an atmosphere of patriarchy that has lingered in the Village despite the attempt to positively address several issues of concern to women. Women complained of abuse from men who misunderstood what their roles should be as husbands when in polygamous marriages, a Yoruba practice that the Traditionalists believe was brought by the orishas. As a result of papers that priestesses presented in 1974, the height of the feminist movement, the Priests' Council (*Igbimolosha*) voted to ban polygamy among those initiated into the movement after that year. Although the women's society (*Egbe Obinrin*) successfully pressed the priests' council for Village rules that would be more accommodating to women as mothers and wives, the priestesses had hit a glass ceiling professionally.[30] They could not be initiated to Ifa, an obstruction confronting women diviners throughout the Yoruba world.

As priestesses to other orishas, women use Merindinlogun system, as do also babalawos where convenient. According to Mary Cuthrell-Curry, there are more women diviners than men in the Western Hemisphere, making Merindinlogun more prominent than Ifa. And, she added, "Merindolugun is much easier to learn than is Ifa."[31] Whereas women are trained as Ifa priestesses (Iyanifas/ Apetibis) in Yoruba communities, they are not fully initiated to Ifa anywhere.

The purpose of training women in Ifa divination is to support the work of the babalawos who often are their husbands, so they always are apetibis whether or not they are iyanifas. Iya Afin, Ayobunmi Sangode, who referred to herself as an apetibii/iyawo Ifa, wrote about their roles:

> [An Iyawo Ifa] must respect her husband and welcome visitors to their house.... She takes care of business for her husband. By respect, every babalawo is her husband.
>
> On every fifth day, which marks the ... day of Ifa, ... the Apetibii [sic] cleans the shrine of Ifa. She washes the wooden tray of Ifa, paints it with white chalk, helps her husband [during divination] and attends to visitors who come to see Ifa. Ojomode is also an Ifa ... day. After cleaning the shrine everyone assembles at the shrine with their kola nut.... Prayers are made and kola given to Ifa. A meal is prepared and the best part given to Ifa with *Iru* stew-beans, sweet.[32]

As indicated in the above passage, priestesses who do so much of the work of the Ifa priesthood during divinations, sacrifices, initiations, and other rituals could not look forward to having careers as Ifa priestesses. The women began to feel that they should not be barred from any part of the Ifa priesthood. They requested initiations, arguing that redactions of female deities Odu and Oshun in Ifa texts had obscured their authentic, original images. At best, the women said, the arguments used by the men to deny women full inclusion were products of sexist, redacted versions of Ifa texts.

Considering the fact that women in Nigeria receive *opele,* the women of Oyotunji should also, they insisted, perhaps not realizing that both *ikin* and *opele* are occasionally are given to women who did not undergo formal initiation rites to Ifa. As I said to my wife about what people receive during initiation rituals, *other than public recognition after an initiation ceremony, you have only what you took into the room.*

Chapter 3

If you had ashe when you went in, you have it when you come out and vice versa. Perceptive babalawos recognize the extraordinary power and authority of an occasional woman and honor that by bestowing upon her divination implements. Some Oyotunji women have that power and authority and deserve to have it honored with bestowing of the title Iyalawo.

Knowing that this topic would be discussed in July, some of the men queried babalawos in Nigeria on the matter prior to coming to the Oyotunji festival and convention. I offered the experience that my wife and I had in Ile-Ife in June (the month before), when she was given a ceremony and presented *ikin* along with me. That presentation entitled her to cast *ikin* to derive Odu Ifa about family matters. It did not make her an Ifa priestess/iyalawo or iyanifa. Speaking to this point, other babalawos said that Nigerian babalawos prohibit women from the Ifa priesthood. One presenter argued emphatically that the position of the Oyo-Yoruba, for example, was quite restrictive of females in the Ifa priesthood and that there are no Ifa priestesses in Nigeria. None mentioned the Odu Ifa verses telling how the female Odu, brought the wisdom from the Supreme Being to earth and how Oshun brought divination. No one asked if women had been robbed of their authority.

For the time being the chiefs and other babalawos concluded that women would continue to play the supportive role of Apetibis, without initiation. Most of the men were adamant in their stand against the women despite the Oba's statement that Christianity and Islam historically were more sexist than ATR. His inference that divination tradition was transformation into patriarchy was, no doubt, too subtle to penetrate the sensitivities of the Oyotunji babalawos. The Ifa priesthood is no worse or better than the

Church that too often denies women participation in its councils of leadership and bars them from the pulpit. Remembered sexist tradition in all faiths is difficult to transcend.

The convention ended on a dismal note, but prospects for a less sexist future for priestesses in Oyotunji arose later that year (December 1992). Priestesses and priests traveled to the Republic of Benin to be initiated into the Dahomean cult of Fa. In 1997, there were two women *bokonon* or full initiates to Fa in the Republic of Benin, which indicates that a mother rights attitude persists among some African Traditionalists.[33] In 2007, there are no iyalawos, only iyanifas and apetibis, and women continue to protest against the discrimination.

If Oyotunji admitted women to the Ifa priesthood, the village's authenticity as Yoruba could be questioned for being unaligned with Ile-Ife in this respect. As an aside from that gender issue, I asked Chief Medahochi about the authenticity of Oyotunji. He stated that he became involved in the Oyotunji-Yoruba Royal Arch Ministry because he was convinced that there is a unique authenticity about Oyotunji. There have been criticisms from outsiders that Oyotunji is "fake" in its architecture, religion, and culture, as well as in the residents and associates calling themselves Yoruba. These judgments generally come from Americans who know virtually nothing about traditional African Religions, cultures and institutions.

As we talked more, I told Medahochi how pleasantly surprised I was to find villages and compounds that looked like Oyotunji in Ile-Ife and elsewhere among the Yoruba in Nigeria. He and I recalled William Bascom's assessment of the village's Yoruba likeness. Medahochi read from the Bascom quote, "What is truly remarkable is the success of the community in recreating, with amazing accuracy, the religion and culture of the Yoruba of Nigeria."[34] Medahochi's satisfied concurrence with Bascom's judgment was mirrored on his continence.

For nearly thirty-five years, the Oyotunji African Village movement has promoted the revival of Yoruba Traditional Religion. Although the Village is centered in that religion, it is fair to conclude that it is intentionally more eclectic, even Pan-African, than the Traditional Religion is in Ile-Ife. The Village has, for example, adopted complementary aspects of Dahomean, elements of Santeria, and rituals from other African Traditional Religions. This is shown in theology/worldview as well as in artistic themes and religious rituals. The New Yorubas don't quibble over the point of whether they are accepted as Yoruba in Africa or in the United States. They assume the posture through their lifestyles and in their hearts and psyches, as well as through a vicarious ancestry.

The significance of Ifa divination in the everyday lives and corporate governance is a hallmark of the Village as it is of Yoruba worshippers everywhere. Realizing the significance of Ifa, Oyotunji aligned itself with Ile-Ife and other Yoruba kingdoms in bestowing upon this orisha the gift of an annual festival. Through the lens of the Ifa Festival in Ile-Ife and Oyotunji, Yoruba religious traditions and cultural practices and values are further explored and assessed.

Oyotunji: African Americans Recover Ifa

Notes

1. Walter King became Nana Oseijeman in 1957 when he Africanized the name "Serge," which he had acquired while studying dance. My summary of Oba Oseijeman's early life is based largely on Carl M. Hunt, *Oyotunji Village: The Yoruba Movement in America* (Washington, D.C.: University Press of America, 1979) and Tracey Hucks' Ph.D. Dissertation: *Approaching the Gods: An Historical Narrative of African Americans and Yoruba Religion in the United States, 1959 to the Present* (Cambridge, MA: Harvard University, 1998).
2. Ibid., 24-25; on other identities, see Amiri Baraka, *The Autobiography of LeRoi Jones/Amiri Baraka* (New York: Freundlich Books, 1984), 215-217.
3. Hunt, *Oyotunji Village*, 22-23.
4. Hunt, *Oyotunji Village*, 27; Amiri Baraka, *The Autobiography of LeRoi Jones/Amiri Baraka* (New York: Freundlich Books, 1984), 205, 215-217, 236 refers to the political party, the Yoruba Temple, and Oseijeman's participation in cultural nationalist activities in New York City; George Brandon, "Sacrifices Practices in Santeria, An African-Cuban Religion in the United States" in *Africanisms in American Culture* (Bloomington: Indiana University Press, 1991), ed., Joseph E. Holloway, 123.
5. Dialogue/interview with Medahochi, as the man initiated to Shango in 1970 is now affectionately known, (Milwaukee, November 17, 1991 and January 1, 1992).
6. From notes from conversations with Medahochi.
7. From Notes of conversations with Medahochi, and Hunt, *Oyotunji Village*, 27.
8. Hunt, *Oyotunji African Village*, 35-36.
9. Ibid., 40.
10. Ibid., 41.
11. Based on conversations with Oba Oseijeman, Medahochi, Toyevi, and Elemosha and from informal sharings of other Oyotunji priests/esses.
12. Hunt, *Oyotunji Village*, 40. Elemosha Awolowo, the first African American initiated into the orisha priesthood by Oseijeman, died in 1990, and his body is interred inside the

Village. Toyevi, the first initiate to Yemoja in Oyotunji, is presently living in Milwaukee.
13. Ibid., 42.
14. Hunt, *Oyotunji African Village*, 50.
15. Hunt, *Oyotunji African Village*, 74-74.
16. Based on notes from conversations with Medahochi.
17. From Discussion/dialogue with Medahochi.
18. Wamue, Grace. "Revisiting Our Indigenous Shrines Through Mjungiki." *African Affairs: The Journal of the Royal African Society*. Vol. 100 (No. 400), 454.
19. This definition is based on readings in C. Eric Lincoln's *Black Muslims in America* (Boston: Beacon Press, 1963), 98-106.
20. From notes of conversations with Medahochi.
21. Find descriptions of egungun masks in Henry John Drewal, John Pemberton, II, and Rowland Abiodun, *Yoruba: Nine Centuries of African Art and Thought*, 24, 176-187.
22. *See Yoruba: Nine Centuries of African Art and Thought*, 175 for translations.
23. Ibid., 178; Babatunde Lawal, "The Living Dead: art and immortality among the Yoruba of Nigeria," *Africa* 47 (1977), 50-61.
24. See Robert Farris Thompson, *Flash of the Spirit* (New York: Vintage Books, 1984), 90.
25. Stuckey, *Slave Culture*, 352.
26. Based on the writer's observations during numerous trips to the village.
27. (New York: Vintage Books, 1984), 90.
28. The term "verbal art" is taken from Richard Bauman, *Verbal Art As Performance* (Rowley, Mass.: Newbury House Publishers, 1977), "Introduction."
29. Charles J. Maland, *Chaplin and American Culture* (Princeton: Princeton University Press, 1989), xvii discusses this trait among folk seeking to reject the dominant culture.
30. The women also organized the Order of Moremi, the legendary Yoruba warrior who infiltrated the warring opposition while they slept. She then poisoned them and won a long-fought battle that was waged against the Yoruba. This is one more national achievement the credit of their fair

Oyotunji: African Americans Recover Ifa

sex, indicating that all of women's savvy and skills should be welcomed in whatever category they are manifested.

31. African-Derived Religion in the African-American Community in the United States," in *African Spirituality: Forms, Meanings, and Expressions,* ed., Jacob K. Olupona (New York: The Crossroad Publishing Company, 2000), 458.

32. *Rites of Passage: Psychology of Female Power* (Brooklyn: Athelia Henrietta Press, Inc, 1999), 74.

33. From conversations with Medahochi in Oyotunji in July 1992.

     On sexism in the Fa Cult, read Edna G. Bay, "The Kpojito or 'Queen Mother' of Pre-colonial Dahomey: Towards an Institutional History," in *Queens, Queen Mothers, Priestesses, and Power: Case Studies in African Gender,* ed., Flora Edouwaye S. Kaplan, (Annals of the New York Academy of Sciences, Vol. 810, June 30, 1997), 19-40.

34. 'Introduction," Hunt, *Oyotunji Village.* Medahochi" had this publication in his possession and read directly from it. Professor Mikelle Smith Omari, who had studied in Oyotunji in 1977, and wrote an article acknowledging its admirable replication in "Completing the Circle: Notes on African Art, Society, and Religion in Oyotunji, South Carolina," *African Arts* 24, No. 3 (July 1991), 66-79.

Chapter 4

The Ifa Festival at Ile-Ife

From priests and reading at Oyotunji, I had learned about Ile-Ife and the Yoruba. Before arriving in the legendary city, I was familiar enough with names of its main characters, mythohistory, language, literature and popular culture to feel as though I was going to my homeland. I had heard about the Ifa Festival, and what I heard was so fascinating that I wanted to experience one for myself—with my wife. Would it be what I envisioned? Would I learn more about Ifa and the traditional history and culture of Ile-Ife? There were insights to be gleaned from attending; an overview of what I learned follows.

The religious significance and pageantry of *Odun Ifa*—the Annual Ifa Festival at Ile-Ife—reaffirmed the significance of Ifa divination as the central dynamic in Yoruba Traditional Religion. It celebrates the immortality of Ifa while sanctifying the harvesting of new yams that coincides with the arrival of the New Year. Ifa Festivals are sacred—but not solemn—occasions filled with prayers, divinations, sacrifices, chants, parades and processions, drumming, dancing and singing. I anticipated an event filled with religious rituals—petitions for cosmic powers to intervene in the realm of human affairs by healing the sick, bringing hope to those in despair, inspiring achievement, and determining if a person is properly pursuing her/his destiny. I expected also that there would be drama and fun—that is that the festival would be an entertaining event. The event fulfilled my expectations.

When I arrived at the Ifa Temple to witness the opening of the festival, I must have looked gullible and ready for spin on the history and culture of Ile-Ife and Ifa. A broad grin and eager continence were spread across my African-American face as I approached the first gathering of Ifa priests. I was festooned in several strands of beads from initiations in Oyotunji to orishas, so the priests in Ile-Ife could presume that I must know just enough to be impressed with their tales about Ifa.

Our visit was anticipated. We were invited while on a brief stay in 1990 and had promised to come in 1992. One after another the priests were prepared to tell us an array of mythic stories. I had heard some of them from the New Yorubas. I had read some from the Ifa verses published by Abimbola, Herskovits, and Bascom. I also had begun to study treatises analyzing mythic and biblical lore while studying for a master's degree in liberal arts at ITC and could analyze them into meaninglessness.

Caught up in the magic of the festival, I tried to lay aside critical reflection and ingest the myths, narratives, and ritualistic wonder of the occasion. I immersed myself in the mythic wonderland for most of two weekends of activities. Yet, I wondered how much of what I saw and heard was fact, possibility, improbability, reality. May be the priest—some educated in college and universities in Nigeria and

The Ifa Festival at Ile-Ife

abroad, some professionals and former Christians. What was I to make of them and their fanciful tales? Perhaps they were men of unquestioning faith, parrots of oral tradition, or beneficiaries (at least vicariously) of miracles. My mind was in a spin, as absorbed and felt overwhelmed by much.

The Ifa Festival evolved out of primal celebrations of divination, but no one seems to know exactly when or other details of its beginning. As mythic memory would have it, the festival has always been. It is continued from the agrarian era of primal celebrations of the fecundity of the soil and its harvest of yams, corn and other life-sustaining crops. The bringing forth of the first fruits from the soil symbolized new beginnings in the cyclically structured universe of the pre-modern Yoruba.

The very name of the festival assures that everyone knows it to be a new yam celebration that occurs in three parts: *Egbodo Ooni* (new yams of the Ooni), *Egbodo Oluwo/Erio* (new yams of the babalawo), and *Egbodo Ife* (new yams of devotees of most Orishas worshipped in Ile-Ife).[1] I treat and refer to the first two festivals in the series as though they are one because of emphasis on Orisha Ifa and he is feted by the Awoni and a host of Ifa priests and their cohorts.

No Ifa Festival begins until after the Awoni pay homage to Osaara at the coconut grove, where the Awoni go with apetibis to gather leaves for the Ifa Festival. They make the pilgrimage to her shrine during the Agbon (coconut) Festival/Odun Agbon,) in early May. Osaara is said to have been one of the wives of Oduduwa and mother of his many children. Legend holds that there was contest to determine who was the greater—Osaara or Olokun, a beadmaker and also Oduduwa's childless wife. Osaara's children were so numerous that when they gleefully and carelessly ran into the assembly, they trampled the jewels that Olokun used to decorate the palace. The myth magnifies the value of children among the traditional Yoruba, indicating that the jewels of the barren woman paled in the presence of the fertile Osaara.[2] Osaara symbolized all mothers whose wealth in children provided working hands for labor-intensive agrarian societies. And moreover, each birth symbolized the recycling of life and people. This tribute to Osaara most likely also is a ritual relic pointing back to primal times, when women were identified with the divination priesthood.

At the end of May, Ifa priests go to *Odo Osaara* (Osaara River) with apetebis to gather Ifa leaves for the Ooni's Ifa (Egbodo Ooni/Erio) rituals. that consist of an array of events. Having taken place near the end of June in the past, this festival now is celebrated annually on the first weekend of June.[3] It lasts over seven days, but the activities of the first five or so days are private and for the benefit of the Ooni and Awoni.

Now, as in more primal times, the festival begins with sacrificing a goat and presenting yams and corn from the first harvest. This ceremony occurs in the sacred Ifa grove near Oke-Itase, the home of the Araba (head and organizational manager of the Awoni). Until recently the highlight of the first day was the building of a thatched temple to Ifa. Then the Awoni would burn it down, using the leaves that thatched the house as fuel for cooking the sacrificial goat. This meant that each year they would have to rebuild the temple to Ifa following the ritual burning and sacrifice that symbolized the cycles of death and renewal.

Impressed with the perceived permanence of Christian buildings around 1950, the Awoni decided to build a more permanent Ifa Temple, where they hold scheduled meetings and have special ceremonies and rituals. This Christian-looking edifice that imposingly overlooks the city from Oke-Itase Hill is the center for the approximately sixteen-hour, public celebration of Ifa.[4] On the outside, the large stone building, with windows but without glass, has a rustic appearance. There is a large assembly room with several columns, a dais, and benches to seat about 500 arranged in rows on both sides of an aisle with folk facing each other and across the back of the room. There are additional smaller rooms, where the Ifa priests hold weekly (every four days) and monthly meetings. The temple has its own generator for operating electric lights and ceiling fans. However, I initially thought the building was the ruins of a deserted church. But if you were fortunate enough to have an informal tour of the temple, as I was, you would find that it still is under construction.

The inside of the temple is structured to focus on Ifa. In the middle of the floor of the assembly room is a stone footprint. Seeing my enthusiasm for the proceedings, a friendly babalawo pointed enthusiastically to the stone and proclaimed, "That is Ifa's footprint!" He told me also that the footprint is located on the very spot on which Orunmila and the sacred palm tree first appeared on earth. In fact, a couple of babalawos repeated this same story to my wife and me. As intrigued as I was by the story at the time of its telling, I reasoned that the claims actually referred to the fact that the Awoni had symbolically incarnated Ifa to establish the significance of the temple.

The supernatural aura acquired in the temple makes it a fitting site for honoring Ifa. I asked where

Chapter 4

they worshipped Ifa before building the temple and was told in the forest and in strategic spots around Ile-Ife. Although the temple now serves some of the functions of the old sacred sites, local babalawos have told me that it is not likely that the forest ever was located where the temple stands today.

The festival is the time for rededicating and re-energizing the sacred palm nuts (ikin) used in Ifa divination. This focus begins in private ritual that lasts six days. The basic pattern of procedure was set by traditional practice. On the first day, the *Awoni* select sixteen leaves from the Ifa grove and bring them to Keji Palace along with new corn from the first harvest. From the corn, they make porridge in which to bury the Ooni's ikin overnight.

On the evening of the third day, the Awoni return to the palace and resurrect the Ooni's ikin from the porridge; then they grind the leaves gathered on the first day in the Ifa sacred grove and place them in cool water with the king's ikin. The Awoni call this ritual "washing Ifa." They place the "washed" ikin in the Ooni's Ifa shrine inside his divining bowl. After they cover the bowl with cloths, the Awoni make offerings and sacrifices to Ifa. Then they place small amounts of blood and meat from the sacrifices atop the Ooni's ikin, leaving it over night.

Later that same evening, the Awoni split a new yam, cover it with palm oil, and take it to the shrine of Esu/Elegba, intermediary between orisha and humans; without whose help no amount of offering or sacrificing would be effective. The meat left over from the sacrifices made at the Ooni's palace is divided among various officials: the Ooni, his wives, other palace and town officials, the Araba, and the Agbonbon (highest ranking spiritual adviser to the Ooni). The rest of the Awoni eat the meat taken from

The Ifa Festival at Ile-Ife

atop the porridge that contained the Ooni's ikin. They imbibe gin from the Ooni's cellars and enjoy the rhythms of a set of four drums known as Ifa drums (*keregidi*). Thus ends the day called "feasting at the palace." From that third evening on, the Ooni and other Ifa traditionalists may eat new yams, which had been forbidden until completion of this ceremony.

Over the fourth and fifth days, the Awoni traditionally rested at their individual homes. On the sixth day, they danced in the market close by the palace, taking turns in a reverse rank order. At night, they returned home, and on the seventh day, they reassembled at the palace and divined for the Ooni, palace chiefs, wives of the Ooni and other people in the palace.[5] They no longer adhere to these traditions as strictly as in former times, as can be determined from their current seventh-day activities.

In present times on the seventh day, the Awoni lead a procession, perform divination, and offer a sacrifice in full view of the public. I witnessed this series of activities in 1992. The opening activity took place on Saturday, June 6 and was called *"Dide si Oke-Itase,"* ("the period of assembly in the Ifa Temple on the Oke-Itase Hill. It lasted about two hours, during which time Awoni, other babalawos and clients, and well-wishers assembled and intermingled. Most were Nigerians from Ile-Ife, Oshogbo, Lagos, Ekiti, Ibadan, Oyo and other Yoruba communities. The English ambassador to Nigeria and his wife, a European-American wife of a Yoruba man, the daughter of a Puerto Rican babalawo and his *ajubona* (the woman who first initiated him into Yoruba Religion in Puerto Rico) had audience with the Ooni. Two African American women were present; they were Miriam Travis (who then was living and working at Obafemi Awolowo University's Library and now lives in California) and one who lived in Lagos and has since died of HIV-AIDS (She allowed her little girl to be trained and initiated as an iyanifa.). My wife and I made four African Americans in attendance.

Since folk already had begun to assemble, the babalawo emcee used a microphone to announce over the din of anticipatory jitters and murmurs that the festival had begun, certainly a necessary electronic intrusion into the traditional event. The crowd consisted mostly of Ifa Traditionalists, including members of the two-to-three-decades-old, *Ijo Orunmila* Adulawo, a congregation of Ifa devotees. The edifice in which the all-night affair was held is accessible to all Ifa worshipers including the members of Ijo Orunmila Adulawo, who have formed a congregation that meets in a church-like assembly, alter traditional Ifa rituals to Christian worship styles, and equate Ifa texts with the Bible.[6] This day of exciting activities began at the Ooni's palace at noon.

The palace activity is a hold over from more traditional times, when the Ooni was thought to be the partly divine ruler, Heaven's ambassador sent to earth to act on behalf of the Supreme Being. The mythical influences on the festival were displayed prominently when the Awoni reenacted the Supreme Being's sending Orunmila to earth. This vibrant ceremony symbolically united the Traditionalists with their king/the Ooni in an effort to maintain, preserve, promote, and praise Ifa.

At approximately 2:00 p.m. "*Lilo si Aafin fun Oro Isurere*" took place. This is a blessing ceremony held in the courtyard of the Ooni's palace and conducted by the Awoni and other babalawos, some of whom were from Oyo and other Yoruba localities. The offices of these sixteen priests were displayed by a line of sixteen prepubescent youths, who carried atop their heads pots wrapped in white cloth that contained Ifa divining instruments. As can be seen in the video clip, the Awoni were resplendently attired and carried the accoutrements of their offices: Beads, chieftaincy medallions designating their respective positions, *Oshun* (Ifa metal staffs with a bird atop them), whisks (with only the Araba carrying two—one in each hand, a sign of his high status), and the Agbonbon wore the Bowler hat with red parrot feathers.[7] After saluting the Araba, the other Awoni joined the Araba, encircling the youths and processing around them.

I was among those in the palace courtyard who received Ifa blessings in this ritual presided over by the Araba. He administered the mixture of herbs with the bluish-white juices from a snail. Since the snail is the animal sacrifice for Obatala, it seemed fitting that it was an opening event to get the festival off to a "cool" beginning. Araba placed the mixture on the navels of the men and boys and above the breasts of the women and girls. Araba said the mixture would strengthen the positive aspects of the personal destinies of those who received it, bestowing upon them calmness, resilience and longetivity.[8] Following this ritual, the Awoni formed a circle that rotated as each of them recited *ese* Ifa (Ifa verses) and saluted the Araba.[9]

As Margaret Drewal emphasized in her study, *Yoryba Ritual*, journey is a major theme in Yoruba festivals and rituals.[10] From 4-7:00 p.m., we participated in *"Lilo si Ojubo Awon Irunmole,"* a procession to sites honoring orishas whose mythic lives are associated with Ifa. The pilgrimage proceeded from the Ooni's palace and winded through traditional sections of Ile-Ife, with the participants stopping at several sacred shrines, including those of Obatala, Oduduwa, and Oranyan. As the Awoni, other devotees and guests processed from shrine to shrine, a company of Ifa percussionists drummed rhythms on keregidi, *pere awo*, and *agogo*, as they danced and sang ceremonial songs, praising Ifa. The *Akoda* (who ranks fifth in the hierarchy of the Awoni and is charged with calling together devotees to the Annual Ifa Festival) danced in the procession to the rhythms of the drums.[11]

Narrations and songs praising the orishas transported participants backward in time to the mythical beginnings of Ile-Ife and the sacred setting of Ifa's world. I found the activities of the Ifa Festival and being in Ile-Ife that I was reminded of Idowu's writing: There were "many stories—entertaining, enchanting, or hair-raising—to tell about its manifold mysteries."[12] I also remembered the Kpojito's mesmerizing stories about the wonders of Ile-Ife and the orishas. The significance of Ile-Ife and the orishas was quickened in my heart and mind.

I was surprised to observe that anyone with facial scarification was banned from entering the Oduduwa Shrine. An Ifa priest who accompanied me throughout the festival was among those so forbidden. While my wife and I entered Oduduwa's shrine, he remained outside. This man explained that he was looked upon as a descendant of Obatala was prohibited from entering the Oduduwa Temple. According to him legend holds that this taboo evolved out of the Oduduwa conquest of the indigenous Obatala peoples whom Orunmila asked to stop scarring themselves. According to Ogundijo, the Oduduwa people had no scarification and guarded their sanctuary zealously against incursions by the scarred Obatala people. This however, was the only shrine at which I observed this type of obvious bias on the grounds of indigeneity. However, he may have aquired these negative feelings about the tradition, there is another explanation.

Since Obatala preceded Oduduwa, Obatala people do not approach the Oduduwa shrine but wait for Oduduwa people to come to Obatala.

It is not surprising that in addition to the pilgrimage to the shrines of the orishas, a journey to the shrine of a revered Awoni was in order. The purpose was to highlight the infusion of the positive spiritual energy of the deceased Araba into the affairs of that day. It also dramatized the interaction between this world and the world of the deceased, whom the Yoruba believe continue to participate in the affairs of the living. The Awoni were there, indicating the importance of the Araba and his family lineage to their organization. This pilgrimage allowed the participants to reflect on the Awoni as an institution energized by spiritual connection to the past, as female family members danced and priests drummed and danced to invoke the spiritual presence and honor the memory of the deceased.

This activity occurred on the grounds of the compound of the *Araba* at the tomb of his father, who was the previous Araba. As chief of the Awoni and son of the deceased, the Araba led the procession and highlighted his own importance. The Araba's position is political and virtually restricted to the matrilineage of Oke-Itase. Ifa priests from other families generally cannot hold the title of Araba. This family is responsible for controlling the Ifa priests whom the Ooni feared would harm him.[13] This is a fear born of ethnic, political rivalries and social tensions that derived from the Oduduwa invasion. This procession ended at the Ifa Temple, where we had a respite.

The next event, *"Akanse Eto"* (Special Activity) began around 7:00 p.m. inside the Ifa Temple. A vibrant procession of dancers in white launched

"Akanse Eto" by ushering in the young female representing the mythical

Odu, the female deity who is closely associated with the coming of knowledge and wisdom from heaven to earth[14] is discussed in Chapter 2. Dressed in white, the woman bore the Ifa divining instruments atop her head in a calabash that was wrapped in white cloth; she presented the calabash to the Araba.

Contradicting redacted myths in the Ifa cannon that Orunmila acquired ikin from heaven, Drewal asserted that he received his implements from his wife, Odu:

> Through his wife Odu, Orunmila got his "sixteen children," that is, the sixteen major divination signs known as Odu Ifa. Odu is represented in ritual by a closed calabash, usually concealed inside a larger container, which a woman carries during rituals.[15]

Through this representation, the male priesthood acknowledges the significance of the female contribution to the origination and maintenance of Ifa. The Awoni and other babalawos used the ikin in the over-night festivities to derive the Odu Ifa for the New Year.

A number of young children who also were dressed in white followed the young woman in the procession. They sang *"Adupe, Odun ya,"* a song that Babatunde Olatunji brought to the United States in the 1950s, rearranged, recorded, and made popular. Following this song, they chanted ese Ifa while performing dances and playing percussions.

As is true of most public events, men (the Awoni) organize the Ifa Festival and the performances that it entails. This is not unusual for among the Yoruba, women tend to play more localized roles within family compounds as organizers of festivals and during them, as with the women dancers at the tomb of the former Araba. This division is a reflection of formalized separations of males and females in traditional Yoruba everyday life as well as in festivals.

Niara Sudarkasa has written about these gendered divisions, arguing that in contemporary Yoruba and other African societies women and men play complementary roles and have dual organization that in reality give their lives social balance.[16] The gendered separation supposes that women's vital, creative force is mysterious and that women are witches. This notion posits the idea that women's powers are virtually uncontrollable and can bring either constructive or destructive influences. Thus, they need to be separated so as not to impose in the male domain the same kind of thinking that denies women membership in the Ifa priesthood.

Aware of Yoruba patriarchal organization of public festivals, I did not find it surprising that women play limited roles in the Ifa Festival. I have noted above, however, that Ifa Festival rituals are preceded by paying homage to the female principle of fertility, as symbolized in Osaara during her Agbon Festival. Women had a presence in the over-night performances of the Ifa Festival. The participation by women of high (chiefs of women's organizations, for example) and of lower status in the performances may indicate their belief in balancing forces in nature for harmony in society.

The Awoni sat apart from all women in one corner of the edifice, indicating their priestly status and officiating responsibilities. Nevertheless, issues of class were implicated in the more equitable seating for some of the women. Female family members and guests of the Araba sat with him on the dais.

Women did have the opportunity to address the assembly during the over-night performances. One woman diviner for the palace of the Ooni was extremely well received. She was a riveting and energetic speaker. Her title is Chief *Iyalodu Agbayeawo Ooni-Ile-Ife*. The yellow and orange colors in her beaded medallion indicate that she is a devotee of Oshun and uses the Merindinlogun system to divine. Her husband accompanied her and stood patiently by her side as she delivered her message, exhibiting himself as the assistant to this revered priestess who knows well Ifa divination verses.

From about 9:00-10:00 p.m., the *"Idupe Odun"* ceremonial performances took place in the temple before the Araba. Every performer or performing group that entered the temple during the all-night ceremonies sent a delegate to pay respect to the Araba by bowing (called *dobale* or *ekunle*, kneeling rites for males and females respectively) before him. By virtue of his position as a representative of the Ooni, the Araba and his entourage (wives, children, relatives special guests and some of the sixteen Ifa priests) sat aside from the masses, elevated on a dais above the rest of the assembly, emphasizing the Araba's high priestly and social rank.

The priests/esses sitting with the Araba, like the *Awise* and Iyalodu, were affiliated with the palace. The awise (a member of the Awoni but not one of the traditional sixteen) was the internationally renowned Ifa scholar Wande Abimbola, who in 1992 was a Senator in the Nigerian legislature and former Vice Chancellor of Obafemi Awolowo University.

Celebrants performing before the Araba consisted of youth groups as well as of their vision. The youth sometimes asked that they be given blessings for the New Year. At one point a member of Ijo Orunmila Adulawo blurted out that one group should not be allowed to participate in the festival because they were dressed in what he identified as the uniform of a Christian Church. He certainly appeared not to have considered the fact that the uniforms of these youths had the Ifa cryptograph of Odu *Ogbe Meji*. The emcee and other babalawo quickly quieted him, and there were no such further outbursts for the rest of the occasion.

The component of the festival that began at midnight carried the descriptive title of *"Itaiji,"* a brief, impromptu talk. The "talks" by babalawos and guests brought greetings and/or treated such subjects as spirituality, admonition to heed Ifa, reminders of blessings that come from adhering to moral and ethical standards imbedded in Ifa texts. These performances seem to have been impromptu with a large measure of improvisational, even jocular, qualities although the sacredness of the occasion is not lost.

The *"Itaiji"* concluded and the period of *"Iwure Pataki"* or petitioning of blessings for the world was welcomed by the audience. This ceremony implies the pan-humanist nature of Ifa tradition. *"Iwure Pataki"* consisted of three major components: (1) *"Fun gbogbo Elesin ni agbaye"* (prayers on behalf of "all religions" in the world); (2) *"Fun Orile-ede wa"* (prayers that focus on Africa and its Diaspora the world over); and (3) *"Ipinnu ohun ti kaluku fe lowo Eleda ninu Odun titun"* (opportunity for attendees to have personal communion with the Irunmoles). The Awoni earlier had made sacrifices in the temple to reinforce the petitions.

From 1-2:00 a.m., the *"Jije Eje fun Eledaa"* ceremony occurred. During this ritual, devotees of Ifa took vows of commitment to continue to maintain and preserve Ifa traditions throughout the New Year. This period brought an announcement that August 20, 1992 was selected via divination as "International African Tradition Day." From 2-5:00 a.m. the *"Ariya Orin, Iyere, Ifa"* ceremony took place. Joyful expressions from Ifa songs, dances, and short speeches by representatives from Ifa Temples in Nigeria and the Diaspora filled this segment of the festival program. I had the opportunity to address the assembly by reciting the Ifa prayer cited in Chapter 2, receiving an enthusiastic response from the audience.

All of the singing and dancing and speaking centered attention on the main reason that the hundreds of folk had come to the festival: to praise Ifa for the harvest and other blessings, to request more blessings, and to "highlight the immortality and eternal powers."[17] Although Omofolabo Ajayi uses this phrase to describe the purpose of the Sanhango Festival, it can be applied as appropriately to the objective of the Ifa Festival.

The rites and ceremonies crescendoed to a high in the latter period of the all-night ritual celebration. This was *"Iwure Ojumo mo,"* the period of praying for blessings. This rite, that is associated with early-morning libations and prayers to Ifa, took place from 5-6:00 a.m. Early morning libations are poured and prayers offered daily by devotees of Ifa at sunrise. During this hour, all the Ifa priests assembled to cast ikin in order to determine what would be the collective destiny of Ile-Ife in the New Year.

The next ceremony, *"Dida Ifa fun Odun Titun Ikede Odu Ifa to hun fun aye,"* took place from 6-7:00 a.m. and consisted of divinations for the world community. Following the announcement of the resultant Odu *Ogbe-Rosun*, Ifa priests employed the traditional call and response method as they recited pertinent Ifa verses.

One of the Ifa priests wrote in cryptogram the Odu for the year, June 1992 through May 1993, in *iyerosun* on an Ifa divining board. The Awoni sent the encrypted powder around for all to eat a pinch if they so chose. The ingesting of the encrypted iyerosun gives one a blessing and protection for the New Year.

Odu *Ogbe-Rosun* spoke to the following issues: Ifa forecasts many blessings and progress for all Ifa adherents. Ifa spoke of wiping his children's hands of loss. Ifa warned that the elders were not adequately taking care of the Irunmoles, and blame was placed squarely on the elders for this neglect. Ifa predicted that barren women would give birth to children that year. Ifa ordered elders to break kola nuts so that children would be kept safe from death. Ifa predicted wealth for the New Year. Ifa declared that adherents should make sacrifice for their mothers and fathers. Ifa admonished devotees to initiate children to Ifa. Ifa said that devotees and other adherents should offer a sacrifice of cooked corn by scattering it in the yard so that the "good" predictions for the New Year would be assured.

After a brief time for refreshing myself, changing clothes, and eating breakfast in the comfortable quarters sponsored by Awolowo University, my wife and I joined a number of folk who had gathered in one of the assembly rooms of the palace around 9:00 a.m. The purpose was to conduct the final ceremony in which the messages from the Ifa divination were conveyed to the Ooni. The presentation was an oration that can only be equated to the plaintive, singing of the blues and anthems simultaneously; the passion filling up those moments and that room was enormously moving for me.

The Awoni had particular instructions from Ifa for the Ooni. These restricted the Ooni's movement for that year. The Awoni offered this advice as protection for the Ooni against possible provocations from the Modakeke settlers who had migrated from Old Oyo to Ile-Ife sometime between 1790 and 1815. For the better part of the twentieth century, there was squabbling between the Yoruba and the immigrants over land ownership, and tensions rose to crisis proportions in the early 1990s. The Awoni said Ifa had warned that the Modakeke people had targeted some people assembled for attack. I never heard that either the Ooni or anyone else had a particular response to the reading. The Egbodo Ooni phase of Odun Ifa ended with *"Lilo si Aafin fun Esa gbigba,"* a ceremony "bidding all to depart into the New Year."[18]

The benefit of being in the company of influential priests, like the Awoni, is that one might be in position to have an audience with the Ooni. Sure enough, just as the group was dispersing for their individual homes on that Sunday morning, the Ooni granted an audience to those of us who were visitors to Nigeria. Our audience with Ooni Adimula Oba Okunade Sijuade included a small delegation of Ifa diviners from Puerto Rico, England's Ambassador to Nigeria along with Miriam Travis, my wife and me.

The second part of tha annual Ifa festivities is Egbodo Oluwo/Erio and like Egbodo Ooni, it is mostly private, reserved for Awoni and Ifa priests to whom he is teacher. This recap is taken from published narratives of this event. As recently as the 1960s, Egbodo Oluwo/Erio was a nine-day affair for Ile-Ife babalawos. The associated rituals gave them the opportunity to visit the Odu pots that they received as Ifa priests and to revitalize their ikin. Keregidi drummers performed Ifa thythms every day, all day, of the nine days in former times. The babalawos went to the temple of Olodu, the building that houses odu (the pots used in their initiations) and remained there for nine nights. On the first day all Ifa diviners in Ile-Ife took divining implements to the grove of Olodu, where babalawos placed ikin in individual containers and filled them with cornstarch porridge made "of new corn and leaves," leaving them to soak overnight.

Each day there followed activities similar to those performed at the Ooni's palace during Egbodo Ooni. On the first day, the babalawo washed the ikin and placed each set in the owner's divining bowl, covered it with cloth, and set it in the Ifa alcove. They offered a blood sacrifice, feeding some to the ikin; they cooked and ate some of the sacrifice with new yams; and they offered yam and palm oil to Eshu/Elegba.

On the sixth day, the babalawos used leaves to cleanse the ikin of blood, and they divined for each other and for the wives (iyanifa) of Ifa and wives and other helpers (apetibis) of babalawos, after which they prayed for blessings. On the seventh day, the wives of Ifa offered the sacrifices prescribed in the Odu Ifa. The babalawos rested on the eighth day. On the ninth day, they sacrificed goats, and touched the head of the sacrificed female goat to the heads of the babalawos, their wives, and children. Babalawos then divined with kola nuts. After a series of divinations, the babalawos gave those present some of the encrypted iyerosun containing figures of the Odu as a blessing.

The babalawos dressed in their finery, replete with the various ornaments and symbols of their respective priestly offices. Before going among the public, each babalawo entered the room that housed the odu pots, moving backward and touching his forehead to the ground before the covered pots. Then each of them "put his . . . [pot] on the head of his son or daughter, a young 'wife of Ifa,' or a young apprentice," who processed with the odu into the street. The babalawo spent a final night at the temple of Olodu. Then the babalawos and their families were prepared to eat the new yams. Not everyone could eat new yams at this time; devotees of some other orishas could not eat them until August as determined by Ifa divinations.[19]

Today's babalawos do not adhere strictly to the nine-day regimen. Feeding and washing ikin and worshipping odu still are conducted privately among the babalawos, but not for as long as the traditional nine days for obvious reasons. A number of babalawos are employed outside the religion in government, education, construction and various kinds of modern careers and do not have the leisure of traditional times to worship and celebrate for extended periods. Probably for this reason, public activities occur on Saturdays and Sundays, allowing clients and priests attached to the several houses headed by the babalawos to participate in ceremonies and hear the odu for that house for that year.[20]

My wife and I had the opportunity to draw out our festive activities by attending the gathering of Ifa priests and clients from the house of the Aseda Awo, Babatunji Adeyefa in the public ritualistic ceremonies. The Aseda's event was one of many, for it is at this time that the Awoni, in their separate community locations, are scheduled to have the final Ifa celebration for the year. The Aseda's celebration took place entirely outdoors, where a string and thatch shrine to

The Ifa Festival at Ile-Ife

Ifa was erected and many of the Ifa sacrifices, prayers, chants, and dances were repeated. Many of the Ifa priests looked familiar to me because they were participants in the Egbodo Ooni/Erio Festival. Children were there in significant numbers.

Similar to the previous festival, this local, public event began with a pilgrimage through the local community. Ifa drummers played during the ceremony, and the Aseda performed in a capacity similar to that of the Araba during Egbodo Ooni. Unlike the Araba, however, who appeared to be presiding ceremonially, the Aseda was the priest performing the rituals. He was actively involved in the divination conducted for the festival and in making the offerings (sacrifices) to Ifa. He led the singing and dancing during every phase of the ceremony.

Although only a dozen or so people attended, this local festival was in fact another intense encounter with an Ifa tradition that lasted several hours that day and into the night.[21] This celebration ended with a feast in the Aseda's home, prepared from the Egbodo Oluwo/Erio ceremonial sacrifices. In a parting statement, the Aseda challenged me, an Ifa priest from Oyotunji, to join the Ile-Ife Ifa devotees in a show of spiritual unity by holding Ifa Festivals. They, of course, already were being held in Oyotunji Village annually although without much fanfare.

It seems to me that the Egbodo Ooni and Egbodo Oluwo/Erio activities have been collapsed into a limited amount of time to cater to modern time constraints of Ifa devotees and supporters. Without this sensitive arrangement, there would be fewer working folk present, and—depending on how far they had to travel fewer out-of-towners would attend.

Chapter 4

By the time that I attended this festival, I had spent years studying Ifa myths, music, and divining, but I never expected to have a divination performed for me upon the occasion of my attending an Ifa Festival. This special treat was afforded me in Ile-Ife in 1992. The Aseda divined for me, and Ifa revealed that my spiritual name is Ikukomi, which means an individual whom "death and evil reject." Only my wife and I knew the significance of the name for me because of an incident that had occurred in my life years before. On September 5, 1969, my brother (Philip) and our wives were celebrating his birthday when our automobile crashed head-on into a tree. I was stunned but not badly hurt. I later came to understand that I had been found without any vital signs and pronounced dead at the scene.

Before ambulances took us away from the scene of the accident, I thought I had gotten up and gone to my brother and our wives and resuscitated the three of them. This could not have been possible according to firemen on the scene that night. I was told later that both my brother and his wife had their heads dashed into the front windshield; they were critically hurt and unconscious. I had been pronounced dead at the scene of the accident taken to the hospital morgue where I regained consciousness, took a cover off my face and body, got up and found my way to the emergency waiting room. I recall startling my mother and sister when they looked up and I was among the living.

This incident flooded my mind when I heard this spiritual name that Ifa presented to me. This is why the Aseda's reading stunned me, for my life had been spared from death, but he had not known about it. I think of myself as also being spared from spiritual death by standing firm on my convictions with respect to the Vietnam War I was fortunate in spite of the fact that I spent years in and out of imprisonment and decades of continued persecution and stress caused by having my military status left unresolved. With the Ikukomi name I received a title, *Oloye Atokun Eegun,* enabling me to study further in order to establish an egungun society from my house in the United States. My responsibilities to the Egun had appeared over the years in divinations.

By the end of the festival, I had collected several songs, particularly from the Egbodo Ooni activities. They represent the variety of interests and problems that were on the minds of festival participants throughout Yoruba traditional history. The mix of contemporary and esoteric Yoruba made translation difficult. I am grateful to have been able to rely on the services of Adebayo Ogundijo for translation support as I worked from the recordings to write out the lyrics. I did tape and video record aspects of the performances throughout the festival. They provide insight into the worldview of Ifa devotees and illustrate the fact that all orishas, which are rooted in the Odus, speak through Ifa. In the festivals you can observe the interaction between Ifa and the other spirit forces in songs as well as in the pilgrimages. Ifa devotees performed these songs and many more during the overnight periods set aside for performance in the Ifa Temple.

1. "*Odun De*" was sung by a children's group. It was made popular in the United States by Nigerian Drummer, Babatunde Olatunji, as noted above.

>   Odun de, Odun de;
>   Odun de, Odun de, Odun yon.
>   Ile ire, e, e, e, e, e, e;
>   Odun de, Odun de.

Verses to this song are improvised, but all of them refer to giving thanks for a fruitful New Year harvest at festival-time.

2. "*Awa o soro*" indicates that ancestral elements are integral to the Ifa Festival even though there were no egungun ceremonies invoking the spirits of the ancestors. Some scholars allege that the orishas are deified ancestors, deified because of their contributions to the development of Yoruba civilization. So any reference to orishas and irunmoles may be thought of as celebrating the spirits of deified ancestors, including Orunmila. As the song below indicates, Ifa worship and its ceremonial traditions were handed down as part of the Yoruba ancestral legacies. This song stresses the importance placed on the intergenerational preservation of Yoruba Traditional Religion.

>Awa o s'oro lo e le wa o;
>Awa o s'oro lo e le wa o.
>Igbagbo o pe, o ee
>Igbagbo o pe k'awa ma s'oro
>Awa o soro lo e ile wa o.

>We will not forget our ancestral traditions.
>We will not forget our ancestral traditions.
>Christianity will not prevent us from remembering.
>Christianity will not prevent us from preserving our ancestral traditions.
>We will preserve our ancestral traditions.

3. "*Orin Ibeji*": This is a song about the importance of children in traditional Yoruba societies as symbolized by twins. It suggests the value of twins as a double blessing. You may recall from reading

in Chapter 2 that the major Odu Ifa come in pairs/twins—male and female. While this song praises the reliability of the palm oil tree, it suggests that the yield from the soil is insufficient to bring forth a variety of staple foods. Fertility and infertility are frequent themes in Ifa verses, always admonishing that blessings come and leave depending on a person's adhere to the wisdom of Odu Ifa.

> Epo m' be ewa m' be - o
> Epo m' be ewa m' be - o
> Epo m' be ewa m' be - o
> Epo m' be ewa m' be - o
>
> Aya mi oja a— o-e,
> Aya mi oja o-e lati bi beeji
> Epo m' be ewa m' be - o
>
> There is palm oil and there is beans.
> There is palm oil and there is beans.
> I'm not afraid to give birth to twin children
> I'm not afraid to give birth to twin children,
> as long as,
> There is palm oil and there is beans.
> There is palm oil and there is beans.

4. "*Orin Oriha Ifa and Ogun*" is a song that focuses on unity between Yoruba deities Ifa and Ogun. This Ifa chant emphasizes the importance of integrity and virtue in life, *iwa pele* (good character).

> Both devotees of Ifa and devotees of Ogun,
> may we not die.
> Both devotees of Ifa and devotees of Ogun,
> may we not die.
> May God not allow us to have children who
> are thieves.

> Cheating does not make human beings
> prosperous;
> God do not allow us to have such children;
> Whether I have earthly father or not, you
> beat me and see.
> You will know that I have a heavenly father.

5. "*Iyeye Leaves*": Like the Ayo game, Iyeye leaves from the sour plum tree, referred to in Ifa verses, are believed to be symbolic of an abundantly fruitful life that will yield a person wealth. This chanter bemoans the fact that one cannot possess wealth or monies equal to the number of Iyeye leaves, which are part of the Ifa Festival apparatus used to cleanse ikin. (Protection against wealth being used for evil)

> The money that I have is not enough,
> The Iyeye leaves are usually 200 in number;
> The Iyeye leaves are usually 200 in number;
> All good things that I have are not enough;
> The Iyeye leaves are usually 200 in number;
> The Iyeye leaves are usually 200 in number;
> I have performed the traditional ritual of
> good that I know.
> The Iyeye leaves are usually 200 in number;
> The Iyeye leaves are usually 200 in number;
> I have not performed an evil ritual of trouble.
> The Iyeye leaves are usually 200 in number;
> The Iyeye leaves are usually 200 in number.

6. "*Agbe*" is a mythical bird that can fly incredible distances. This song employing Orunmila to protect one's home while s/he is away is a prayer for the traveler to have a safe return home, hence: "we do not travel to a foreign land without returning home."

> Agbe fly me home;

> Agbe fly me home.
> We do not travel to a foreign land
> without returning home.
> Agbe fly me home;
> Agbe fly me home.
> We do not travel to a foreign land
> without returning home.

> "Orunmila Watch Over My Home;"
> If I go to a foreign land,
> Orunmila, watch over my Home.
> If I go to a foreign land,
> Orunmila, watch over my Home.

7. "*If I Ever Come Back*" is a song indicating that life is best when lived in harmony with the orishas. It is a commitment to Ifa cultural tradition. The traditional belief in the recycling of life is expressed.

> I'm not kidding, I say I'm not kidding;
> I'm not kidding, I say I'm not kidding;
> If I ever come back to the world again,
> I will be a devotee of the divinities.
> I'm not kidding, I say I'm not kidding;
> I'm not kidding, I say I'm not kidding;
> Whenever I am reborn,
> I will be a Traditionalist,
> a devotee of the divinities.

These songs were performed in the African traditional call and response. Virtually all of them were accompanied by Ifa rhythms and dance movements and were sung with high energy and great harmonizing of female, male, and children's voices, as can be observed in the video footage in the writer's archive.

My first encounter with the Ifa Festival in Ile-Ife, much like my first Ifa divination in Oyotunji, deepened my spirituality. Yet, I realized that this religious occasion had not been sanctimonious. In this regard, Omofolabo Ajayi's observations on Yoruba festivals is *apro pos* for the Ifa Festival:

> Although closely associated with a particular deity, the festival goes beyond a mere religious celebration; it truly becomes, . . . "the great artistic institution" of Yoruba people. In its realization, the religious origin or foundation becomes very easily superseded and the festival is turned into a "carnival, dance drama or ritual drama."[22]

Certainly, I had witnessed representations from dance, rhythms, singing, and the spoken word but also sculpture, masonry, painting, beadworks and wearing apparel. Throughout the afternoon and evening hours, a marketplace displayed yet more artistic creations for sale. I had been entertained and my soul had been touched with a new and harmonious beginning for life with Ifa.

It was with amazment that I observed that the Awoni and other Yoruba traditionalists portrayed in festival aspects of the history and culture that I had derived from my studies. I saw that they continued to preserve, albeit in redacted versions, the spiritually rich Ifa canon and the transformed Yoruba cultural legacy. Until the Sixties this knowledge and culture were virtually lost to African descendants in North America. I left Nigeria believing that the Ifa Festival holds keys for enriched insight into Yoruba Traditional Religion and the history of Ile-Ife. Knowing that an Ifa Festival was scheduled for July in Oyotunji, I wondered how much of the Ile-Ife experience I could relive in the United States.

Notes

1. The third yam festival is Egbodo Ife; it occurs in August and ushers in the time for devotees of other orishas to eat new yams; William Bascom wrote about this in *IFA DIVINATION: Communication Between Gods and Men in West Africa* (Bloomington: Indiana University Press, 1969/1991), 99; Wande Abimbola also wrote about Egbodo Ife in *Sixteen Great Poems of Ifa* (UNESCO and Abimbola, 1975), 7.

    Margaret Thompson Drewal published a study on festivals and other spectacles in *Yoruba Ritual: Performers, Play, Agency* (Bloomington: Indiana University Press, 1992), from I drew useful insight for this manuscript.

2. My summary description of Asaara is based on the insightful presentation of the festival and dance named her honor by Omofalabo S. Ajayi, *Yoruba Dance* (Trenton: Africa World Press, 1998), 205-214.

3. Chief Michael A. Fabunmi, *IFE: The Genesis of [the] Yoruba Race*, Ikeja, Lagos: John West Publications, Lt., 1985), 94, 147, 186-187 and Ifa priests in Ile-Ife.

    For a for a listing of festivals in Ile-Ife, including Ifa Festivals (*Egbodo Ooni* and *Egbodo Erio*), refer to Chief Fabunmi, *IFE*, 95.

4. William Bascom, *IFA DIVINATION: Communication Between Gods and Men in West Africa* (Bloomington: Indiana University Press, 1991), 95-96; the date for the construction of the Ifa Temple building is from Chief Meyegun 'Bayo Ogundijo.

5. This is a summary of Bascom's reconstruction of Ifa Festival activities, Ibid., 95.

6. *Orunmila* is a publication of *Ijo Orunmila*.

7. Description of attire is based on observations, video footage accompanying this book, and Bascom, *IFA DIVINATION*, 95.

8. Ajayi, discusses the coolness of movement in the Obatala Dance in *Yoruba Dance*, 69-76.

9. For further discussion of this, read Bascom, *Ifa Divitation*, Chapter X.

10. Refer to "The Ontological Journey" in Drewal's *Yoruba Ritual*, 29-47.
11. Fabunmi, *IFE: The Genesis of [the] Yoruba Race*, 99 was helpful for explaining the role of the Araba as an Awoni.
12. E. Bolaji Idowu, *OLODUMARE: God in Yoruba Belief* (New York: Wazobia, 1962/1994), 11.
13. Bascom, *IFA DIVINATION*, 93.
14. This myth is based on C. Osamaro Ibie, *IFISM: The Complete Work of Orunmila* (Hong Kong: Design Printing Co., Ltd., 1986), 14-16. For additional documentation on Arugba in Yoruba myth, find a photograph of a Shango altar bowl bearing her image in Rowland Abiodun, "Understanding Yoruba Art and Aesthetics: The Concept of Ase," *African Arts* 27, No. 3 (July 1994): 71. The Oshogbo-Yoruba's comparable myth of Oshun is cited in Diedre L. Badejo's essay, "Oshun-Seegesi" in *Dialogue and Alliance*.
15. Yoruba Ritual, 73.
16. Refer to "'The Status of Women' in Indigenous African Societies," in Rosalyn Terborg-Penn, Sharon Harley, and Andrea Benton Rushing, eds., *Women in Africa and the African Diaspora* (Washington, D.C.: Howard University Press, 1989), 25-41 and Mary E. Modupe Kolawole, *Womanism and African Consciousness* (Trenton, N.J.: Africa World Press, 1997).
17. A phrase borrowed from Omofolabo S. Ajayi, *YORUBA DANCE: The Semiotics of Movement and Body Attitude in a Nigerian Culture* (Trenton, N.J.: Africa World Press, Inc, 1998, 86.
18. Fabunmi, *IFE: The Genesis of [the] Yoruba Race*, 116-119 on the Modakeke.
19. Bascom writes about Egbodo Oluwo/Erio in *Ifa Divination*, 96-99; also based on writer's observations.
20. Writer's observation during Egbodo Oluwo/Erio, after receiving ikin from the Aseda Awo.
21. Photographs from this festival are in the Appendix.
22. Ajayi, *Yoruba Dance*, 45.

Chapter 5

"A Time of Destiny": Celebrating Ifa in Oyotunji

I had returned from the Ifa Festival in Ile-Ife about two weeks earlier when I attended the Ifa Festival in Oyotunji in 1992. This gave me useful perspective from which to compare the two celebrations. That year the village was celebrating its 20th anniversary and holding its biggest festivities. The festival convenes annually on the weekend of July 4th—vacation time for many who attended—and is held in conjunction with the Oyotunji National Convention. "A Time of Destiny" was the theme for the 1992 event. The theme signified that the divine destiny of the African Americans was upon them, i. e. that the time to reclaim the African heritage was eminent. This call to destiny was in the forefront of all deliberations and activities for that weekend.

As the babalawo and priests of other Orishas and their families arrived one by one and in small groups, the atmosphere had all the excitement and joy of a homecoming. Folk who regularly did not visit the

Chapter 5

village came in 1992 in recognition of the milestone anniversary. There was quite a gathering from various parts of the United States. People began arriving on the eve of the Fourth of July. Early the next morning they assembled to eat breakfast in the Oyo Horseman—a grill located just inside the Village gate. Others went to the Village marketplace while waiting for registration to begin later in the morning.

This opportunity to fellowship prior to the formal opening was similar to that in Ile-Ife when Ifa priests and supporters were arriving. The priests at Oyotunji introduced themselves to each other or enthusiastically greeted those with whom they had been acquainted for years and engaged each other in conversation. I and other Ifa priests enjoyed several hours of intermingling prior to the official opening. Almost everyone in attendance was African American.

The necessary animal sacrifices had been made by Oyotunji's resident priests on the evening before, out of the public view. This was quite sensible considering the denigration and legal hassles that often are generated in the United States by hearing of animal sacrifices. I was one of the babalawos invited to participate in offering the sacrifices, but feeling the need to rest after driving more than twelve hours, I respectfully declined the invitation. Ifa divination was the method via which the priests had determined what should be sacrificed and how much in order to be assured of having a successful festival and convention.

Another activity that preceded the convening of the festival was a colorful "Elegba parade and Dance of the 'Odu,'" which occurred in the courtyard of Oba Oseijeman's compound. The king referred to "Odu," briefly and cryptically, calling it extremely mystical but not mentioning it as a preserve of males initiated to Ifa.[1] The Elegba dancers were female and male.

"A Time of Destiny": Celebrating Ifa in Oyotunji

Both dressed in raffia skirts, insinuating the sexual themes generally attributed to Elegba. It was fitting for the Ifa Festival to be preceded with an Elegba ceremony. As the spiritual companion to Orunmila, Elegba could clear the way for blessings to come to the festival. Following this opening event, there was about an hour respite, permitting the devotees to other orishas as well to Ifa—and their guests—to continue to greet each other.[2]

At noon *"Je 'Fa e ku joko babalowo lori eni"* ("seating of the babalawo on the mat for divination") preceded the formal opening of the festival. It convened in the Obatala Temple in Oba Oseijeman's compound. Inside the temple are the sacred ornaments and symbols representing Obatala, making it a reasonable location for the Oba and other babalawo of Oyotunji to come to consult Ifa. The divination encompassed not only the weekly Ifa reading for Oyotunji but also provided readings on the festival and convention.

Divination and debate among the all-male cabal of Ifa priests continued in this location for several hours. The debate centered around two major issues: (1) the establishment and indigenization of Ifa initiation rites in Oyotunji and the estimated costs of such rites and (2) women's initiation into the Ifa priesthood. The issue of established and indigenized Ifa initiations was settled in the affirmative, giving the nod to the New Yorubas' self-identity of uniqueness that set them apart from traditional Yoruba of Nigeria. The matter of women's roles in the Ifa priesthood was not resolved during the divination ritual and continued as a topic later, during the convention part of the festival. Renewed discussions would be held in abeyance until later in the weekend.

Oba Oseijeman and other Obatala priests convened the festival by pouring libations and praying for and blessing all in attendance. This was similar to the invocation and anointing by the Araba at Ile-Ife's Ifa Festival opening. Following this ritual the proceedings turned quickly into an assembly over which babalawos presided. They gave prepared lectures and impromptu talks, discussing issues pertaining to the Ifa Movement in North America. Convention discussions were born of the insecurities of a priesthood that constantly grapples with its validity as an authentic Yoruba movement in the Diaspora. The members of the assembly wondered, e. g., whether the Oyotunji initiation of males even into the Ifa priesthood is accepted by the priests at Ile-Ife.

Not having previously attended an Ifa Festival in the village, this was the first time that I had been publicly recognized as a babalawo in Oyotunji village since my 1986 initiation. The Oba announced my membership in the Oyotunji Royal Ifa Academy. There was elation when I told them that my Ifa divination in Ile-Ife revealed that I already was an Ifa priest. The Oba was pleased to hear that an Ifa priest in Ile-Ife had acknowledged the validity of my initiation that had taken place in Oyotunji.[3] Many Ifa priests from Oyotunji went to Yoruba communities in Nigeria to be initiated so that they could feel more assured of legitimization. One of the exceptions was Medahochi, who led the push for indigenization by African Americans.

The next event, a performance honoring ancestors (an egungun ceremony), was a radical departure from anything I had experienced in the Ile-Ife, Ifa Festival, where no egungun appeared. This egungun ceremony took place around 2 p.m. and featured a masked dancer to whom the Alaagba (Chief Olofundeyi Olaitan, the man dressed in white in the accompanying video) referred as Egungun 'La, the embodiment

"A Time of Destiny": Celebrating Ifa in Oyotunji

of the "Dancer from Heaven's Courtyard" or ancestral dancers from Heaven. Egunguns were appropriate in Oyotunji's Ifa Festival because of the significant role of the enslaved African ancestors in giving African Americans linkage to the continent. The Alaagba explained that "Egungun 'La" is petitioned annually during the Ifa Festival for blessings and leadership in the movement to revive the African ancestral heritage, as discussed in Chapter 4.[4]

In Oyotunji, the egungun ritual began with a moving processional that featured ceremonial musicians, including players of West-African *sakara*, *dundun* and other West African drums, and agogo and *shekere* players. When "Egungun 'La" began to process, it was guided by one female (Iya Ato) and one male (Atokun) priest while everyone joined in the egungun welcoming song:

> E e egun de ajuba tomboye
> E e egun de ajuba tomboye.[5]

Although the Alaagba is chief and presides, the Iya Ato, the only female member of the society, is owner and care taker of the egungun cloth. She is responsible for overseeing the attire and appearance of these masked dancers.[6]

The egungun society is dominated by males in Oyotunji as well as in Ile-Ife in contemporary times, yet Ifa literature suggests that there was a time when women controlled this ancestral rite and owned its sacred symbol, the egungun cloth. The Iya Ato's role apparently is a relic from that mythic time. A narrative of women's descent from and men's ascent to that leading role is told in the myth of "Iyami" (my mother).[7]

The egungun rite during the festival is an example of Oyotunji's innovation on an Ile-Ife ritual. Unlike the Ifa Festival in Ile-Ife, Oyotunji brings Ifa and egungun together in performance. Yet, as with every other facet of traditional Yoruba life, the egungun rites depend on divination, and the Ifa oracle must have pre-sanctioned this programmatic order.

Oba Oseijeman and three of his wives gave offerings of fresh fruit and performed the "Funga" dance of welcome before Egungun 'La. The last segment of the egungun rite was similar to the "Itaniji" period of festivities during the annual Ifa Festival in Ile-Ife, for it featured an address by community leaders. In the Oyotunji instance, there was a "Special talk on Awareness."

Only one person talked during the egungun ritual; that was the alaagba. He stated that there will be dependence on ancestral wisdom and knowledge as black folk try to fulfill their national destiny. He made the talk practical for folk unfamiliar with Yoruba Traditional Religion, saying that preparation for fulfilling one's destiny includes knowing the foods, behaviors, social relations, and vocations that allow a people to live harmoniously with forces in nature and society. When Ifa priests publicly cast ikin to derive odu, they again stressed this point. They reminded representatives of the Black community that after descendants of Africa lost direct contact with the continent, they also lost awareness of egungun (how ancestral spirits could be invoked) as well as with other sacred ancestral traditions. Because of these losses, the villagers believe that the most positive move African Americans can make is backward to retrieve the knowledge and wisdom of their African cultural past. Alaagba said, Black folk must "go backward to go forward."[8]

"A Time of Destiny": Celebrating Ifa in Oyotunji

Alaagba continued to speak, saying: Like the Yoruba and their descendants everywhere, members of the Oyotunji Movement believe in eternal life, for though the physical body expires, the spirit lives on forever. Yoruba Traditionalists, like those at Ile-Ife, believe that these remembered ancestors react to deeds committed by the living and send, from the spirit world, blessings for deeds creating harmony and curses for those causing disharmony. This is in tune with Yoruba traditional belief that the community consists not only of the living but also of the dynamic spirit of the dead so long as their names are remembered. By invoking names of the deceased, the living are reminded of the personality and social contributions of the deceased, who most likely had been an elderly.

The purpose of egungun is for surviving relatives to periodically seek the spiritual presence of the "living-dead," (those ancestors still in the memory of the living).[9][10]

The Alaagba informed his listeners that talking about their ancestral traditions was not enough. He urged them to construct ancestral shrines in their homes so as to establish a place for calling the names of their ancestors, offering them fresh water, flowers, incense, and other favorite things. He told them to burn candles so that the living family members would be united with the eternal flame of life. This flame and other gifts, according to the priest, would provide the reverent one immediate access to the spirit world of the ancestors, providing a solid building block toward identifying and reclaiming African traditions. Such a move would allow African Americans to build African-centered traditions within the United States.

The Egungun 'La rite is included in the Ifa celebrations at Oyotunji partially because there are few times in which numerous Ifa devotees and supporters assemble in the village. Public events such as the Ifa Festival provide an opportunity for the Oba and other priests to recall the power of ancestors. It is through events such as these that there is opportunity to try to inspire folk beyond the Village to embrace African religious traditions.

In a talk later that day, the Oba commented on the significance of what he called "ancestor worship." He asserted, "When worshipping ancestors, you worship your own genetic makeup."[11] He said he based this statement on biogenetic theories that each human is the sum of all past ancestors. More than anything else, then, the egungun ritual provided a "symbolic experience" which held "forth its particular kind of information [through the medium of] ritual." The "symbolic experience" became a moment in which the "formal teaching of the [Yoruba/Ifa] culture was transmitted"[12] through integrative activity that included singing, visual spectacle, dance, oration.

The egungun ritual ended with the masqueraders being escorted out of the courtyard and into the forest, while the participant-observers sang as they waved good-bye:

> A a a a-tomboru
> A a a a-tomboru
> A a a a-tomboru-o[13]

At 5:00 p.m. children of Oyotunji's Yoruba Royal Academy performed, reminding me of the dancing, drumming, singing done by youth groups during the sixteen-hour celebrations at the Ifa Festival in Ile-Ife. It is interesting to note that these young students of Yoruba religion are required to be formally educated while simultaneously being trained in ancestral tradi-

"A Time of Destiny": Celebrating Ifa in Oyotunji

tions of the Yoruba. Most of them are astute performers, having begun their training at very early ages.[14]

The 8:00 p.m. session included a toast to the Alaagba of Ile-Ife, the representative of the Ooni to the Awoni. Next those assembled saluted the flag and the Oba of Oyotunji. This ceremony was held in the courtyard of the Ogboni-Shango Temples in the Oba's compound. It fulfilled the requirement that members of the Oyotunji Movement affirm their recognition of the village as an extension of Ile-Ife and its leadership.

Although there is no Ifa priesthood equivalent to the Awoni of Ile-Ife, there are priests who have Awoni titles. Medahochi, for example, was Aseda to the Oyotunji Ifa priests. There are a number of chiefs, and several were present; as a group, they reaffirmed their oneness with Oyotunji and their commitment to the Oba.

Following these mostly political preliminaries, the Oba addressed the gathering. The Oba's talk dealt primarily with the significance of Oyotunji and its place within the culturally diverse United States. He had two major themes: African American identity and the nature of Ifa.

About the African American identity, he said: Africans in North America are in fact aware that they have African origins, but the vast majority of them are not aware of the customs and traditions of their ancestors. Many African Americans are searching for techniques that would reconnect them to their ancestral traditions. The celebration of Kwanzaa is only one avenue by which African Americans seek to identify with their lost African traditions. Oyotunji has motivated African Americans to acquire African names and attire and to adopt African concepts and languages. Even African-American Muslims and Christians have observed the need for and the obligation to reclaim and revitalize African traditional knowledge that was severed from them during their sojourn in the Diaspora.

The Oba asserted that the American capitalistic values that form the basis of the economic exploitation of Native Americans and African Americans needs to be challenged. He expressed the view that Ifa tradition is a source from which African descendants in the United States can begin to find solutions to the socioeconomic disinheritance inflicted upon them by the oppressive capitalistic system.

The Oba recited a litany of Yoruba beliefs. Responses to the litany indicated that, like their Yoruba antecedents, the New Yorubas accepted the notion that everything in the universe has a divine purpose. Ifa provides knowledge and wisdom necessary for allowing people to resolve troubles, self heal, and know reasons for their existence. Ifa is the significant key for unlocking and understanding individual and corporate destinies. Through Ifa, African Americans could become aware of African traditional rituals that can help them acquire more productivity and harmony in their lives. The Ile-Ife Ifa priests also taught about Ifa but not as didactically. The priests in Ile-Ife taught through parables, mythic storytelling, and other dramatic performances.

Oba Oseijeman criticized what he perceived to be the Christian and Muslim patriarchal notion of the Supreme Being as male despite the recent disavowal of that principle in progressive Christian circles. Oyotunji espouses the idea, the Oba explained, that God is neither male nor female but rather an unknowable supernatural force that permeates all existence. He described Olodumare as being energy,

"A Time of Destiny": Celebrating Ifa in Oyotunji

not an anthropomorphized character. He advised listeners not to be idolatrous, saying what religious people are when assigning human characteristics to the Supreme Being.

Addressing the myriad issues and troubles facing African Americans, the Oba continued: Oyotunji has established its own institutions of theological education for the training of priestly scholars. By being academically prepared and spiritually attuned to Ifa knowledge and wisdom, these priests are able to address effectively issues of self identity and social disinheritance. In so doing, they hope to eventually lead African Americans in improving their spiritual and social lot.

On the following day (Sunday), the assembled babalawos, prepared to chant verses from the sixteen major Odu Ifa. This ceremony did not begin, however, until after devotees of Ifa, other priests/esses, and visitors had fully assembled and taken part in a pilgrimage to orisha shrines in the Village. The contingencies paraded throughout the village, marching in cadence to rhythms of the drummers, while singing songs of praise at the orisha shrines. This was a reminder that all orisha are contained in Ifa. This pilgrimage to shrines was reminiscent of my similar processional experience in Ile-Ife.

One of the most curious of the shrines visited during the Ifa Festival is that of the ancestor Kpojito Omiyale Hwesihuno, who was in Oyotunji when I first visited in 1972. As stated in Chapter 3, she had taken the Fon title Kpojito after moving to Atlanta. She lived in both Sheldon locations after being initiated and was the eldest person to establish residency on the site of the present Village. Following the burial on the Oyotunji premises of Chief Elemosha (the first person to be initiated by Oba Oseijeman in

Chapter 5

South Carolina), there was such disharmony during egungun ceremonies that Ifa had to be consulted. Some have reckoned that the Kpojito could not reconcile her not being memorialized or buried at Oyotunji after Chief Elemosha's burial there. To discern more about this conflict, Oba consulted Ifa.

The divination revealed that the Kpojito should be enshrined as a patron ancestor of Oyotunji. She was to be revered as a pioneer who helped found the Village and who became the first Chief Priestess of the Yemoja Temple there. The divination stipulated that Kpojito was to be paid homage in a special ceremony annually during egungun ceremonies in order for the Village to maintain spiritual harmony among residents.

As I stood before that shrine on that spot where she had lived in the village and where I had visited her many times, memories flooded my mind. I recalled her contributions to me and to the lives of others. A number of Atlantans—some of who now are judges, lawyers, professors, movie actors, acclaimed craftsmen—received elekes of their personal orishas and Yoruba sacred names from Kpojito. It was a direct result of her teaching that two young African American males—Tosu Tosasalem and I—were initiated into the Dahomean religious system and taken through priestly rites that entitle us to practice Fa (and Ifa) divination.

The Kpojito was committed to preparing young priests. She worked with Oyotunji's first Shango initiate—Shangodele Omowale (Medahochi) to assure that Tosu and I memorized verses from the sixteen Fa Du, their corresponding sacrifices, and methods of manipulating and reading implements of Fa/Ifa divination. I inherited her two volumes of the first publication of *Dahomey*. My appreciation for the learning and engagement with Fa under both she and Medahochi inspired me to attend the Ifa Festival in 1992.

Performance of Odu Ifa by the babalawos occurred outdoors, at a podium that was sheltered from the blazing, South Carolina, summer sun. Elegba masqueraders flanked the podium on both sides. Folk sat in three groupings during this ceremony: The Oba and babalawos, wives of the Oba and priestess wives of babalawos, and visitors.[15] As priestly leader of the Oyotunji community, Oba Oseijeman began the series of performative readings. After he had invoked the presence of Ifa, the Oba (who has memorized scores of Odu) recited in Yoruba, followed with English translations, the first of the major Odu Ifa—*Iwori Meji* (as seen in the video accompanying this book). Immediately following his chant, his wives sang to Ifa/Orunmila and danced in choreographed steps. They paraded between the readings, circling the palace courtyard as they danced and chanted to several of the orishas represented in the Odu Ifa.

One song was to Oshun, who is transformed from chief diviner to virtually an apetibi to Ifa in redacted Ifa texts.

> Oshun ye ye mi-o;
> Oshun ye ye mi-o;
> Apetibi Orunmila;
> Oshun ye ye mi-o.[16]

At least one of the Oba's wives, Iya Orite, had assisted him in initiating babalawos. Nevertheless, she could not initiate men into the Ifa priesthood because she had not been given the rite of receiving Olodu, a male preserve according to that priesthood's policies. This policy also disallowed her the privilege of receiving

Ifa, so she danced with the other wives of/apetibis to Ifa.

No matter what the limitations of their knowledge of and familiarity with the Ifa canon, all of the assembled babalawos read the Ifa verses in Yoruba, with varying degrees of fluency and facility in tonality. The exercise of reciting and reading Odu Ifa served the purpose of urging familiarity with content of the verses and the archaic language. The dual functions of edifying the audience and of displaying skills in reading and interpreting Ifa texts were served.

As the babalawos performed, they adhered to the formulae of the texts, stating the problems cited and the specified sacrifices that would help bring resolution. They sometimes ended a performance with words of encouragement from Ifa, as for example: "If you want to do something, Orunmila says make a sacrifice and you will be able to do it." Another read: "I am the babalawo of the town; I am the physician of the town." At predetermined intervals the women performed a pantomime, acting out the myth of Orunmila and other deities who climbed down the great chain from heaven to earth.

One of the final chants was to ori, the head as symbol of each individual's sacred destiny. Ori is thought by Yoruba Traditionalists to be the abode of every individual's wisdom and knowledge. That's why they salute ori, the mark of destiny—their imprinted compass to life and beyond—in song:

> Ori O' lami;
> Ori O' lami;
> Obatala, Orunmila;
> Ori O' lami, Baba.

Roughly translated this means:

"A Time of Destiny": Celebrating Ifa in Oyotunji

> Guide me destiny;
> Guide me destiny;
> Obatala, maker of humans;
> Orunmila, keeper of destiny;
> Guide me destiny.

A chant to Babaluaiye (earth father), asking for their prayers to be answered, followed.

> E e e pa
> E pa baba, E pa-o.[17]

Thus, the singers prayed that the earth deity would accept, on behalf of all of the orishas represented in *Odu Ofun Meji*, their chanted offering. At the end of this final performance, they recited the words, *aboru, aboye, agbosi se-o*. This signaled the end of the recitation of Ifa verses.

After brief, closing comments, the Oba and his chiefs took their leave. As Ifa priests, they appropriately were followed closely by two Elegba priests—most devout allies of Ifa. The king's processional song by the Oba's wives signaled other courtiers and guests that the Oba was leaving the courtyard. Everyone knew to stand clear of the passage through which he would walk in route to his quarters:

> T'omba s'ile, T'omba s'ile, Oba;
> T'omba s'ile, T'omba s'ile, Oba.
> T'omba s'ile, Tomba s'ile Oba.[18]

After the Oba had a respite, the convention started around 2 p.m. in Igbimolosha Hall near the Oba's compound. This convention was another innovation on the Ile-Ife Ifa Festival. It was presided over by the Ifa priests. Procedurally the convention was patterned after academic and other scholarly forums. It consisted of two main parts: the presentation of papers followed by questions and reactive comments. As mentioned above, the primary issue was whether women should be initiated to Ifa and what should be their roles in the priesthood. After several hours, the convention ended without satisfactory resolution for the women, as discussed in Chapter 3.

The indigenization of the Ifa system was an issue raised during the convention by Medahochi. His thinking is framed by the fact that he always has tended to think and practice innovation and indigenization. Recall, e. g., the conferring of Ifa titles with scoops of cryptographed soil—followed later with his presenting the initiates opele chains for divination? Medahochi suggested that diviners in the United States adopt a native nut or berry as part of their divination utensils in order not to be hampered by the occasional inaccessibility of Nigerian ikin, that had to be transported from Africa. Nationalistic-minded people often turn to indigenization so that they utilize native resources and give them selves distinction.

There are examples of indigenization in religions of the world; I will point out two instances because I think that they are interesting. One is the indigenization of the elements of Communion by members of the United Methodist Church in Tonga (South Pacific). Instead of using grape wine to symbolize the blood of Jesus, they substituted coconut juice and used the meat of the coconut for bread.[19] The rationale behind this was discussed in a paper, presented by a Tonga United Methodist pastor, titled, "Coconut Theology." The Aseda of Ile-Ife quickly saw reasons for innovation when he came to the United States in 1994. Observing that folk live in apartments and that

"A Time of Destiny": Celebrating Ifa in Oyotunji

some products used in sacrifices could be purchased, he wondered if blood from packaged meats could possibly be used to make sacrifices.

Medahochi's additional point that Ifa priests in the United States should receive their validation from the priestly order established on this continent received a bemused hearing. At one level that already happens. Yet, there is the tacit understanding that a babalawo might not be quite authentic until he goes before Ifa priests in Africa. Oseijeman has been among that number with this thought. It comes as no surprise, therefore, that he took several priests and priestesses to the Republic of Benin to be initiated to Fa in 1992.[20] A number of the males already had been initiated to Ifa. The Oba presided over their initiations in Oyotunji and had presented them certificates as babalawos without the presence of any African priests.

Yet, the Oba thought it was necessary for the African American babalawos to be validated on the African continent. He did not want Oyotunji to be misjudged an African American movement without links to the Yoruba communities in Nigeria because of where its babalawos were initiated. He was aware of one of the first questions that people who know about the Village ask: Is Oyotunji authentically African? Oseijeman was afraid that only Africans practicing the traditions and initiating Ifa priests would vouch for Oyotunji's authenticity as a Yoruba movement. Throughout his lifetime, he sought acknowledgement from Ile-Ife as the Village's spiritual homeland. The 5-7 p.m. hours of pouring libations and offering prayer ended the festival.

At the conclusion of the festival, I asked Medahochi with whom I had spent most of the four days of the Ifa Festival, "In what sense is Oyotunji unique, not simply authentic, since the Yoruba have a long tradition of orisha worship and Ifa tradition?" Medahochi answered: In Brazil, they have Candomble, they have Para, and they have Umbanda, they have Macumba, and they have Shango in Trinidad. They have Vodun in Haiti and Santeria in Cuba. He asked and answered, what is unique about Oyotunji Orisha Vodun Religion? "It is unique in that it is the only aspect of North American African tradition that has completed the circle. It is primarily an African institution. It does not rest upon, nor is it incumbent upon, nor dependent upon Catholicism or Catholic spiritualism [as the others are]." Medahochi explained that Oyotunji is based primarily on an indigenous African tradition. Notwithstanding the fact of innovations and syncretisms, the religion of the Oyotunji Yoruba is a revivification of the Yoruba Traditional Religion.

This point was brought out in an article written by Mikelle Smith Omari, who earned a Ph.D. from UCLA and returned to visit Oyotunji in March and April of 1989, after having studied there in 1977.[21] One of her published articles provides a rejoinder to the question that I had put before Medahochi:

> [Oyotunji is] a New World model sufficiently similar to the prototype to merit official sanction from Ile-Ife.... Oyotunji must be viewed not only as an educated, organized, general manifestation of resistance to mainstream Euro-American society but more specifically as a part of a global phenomenon of maintenance of traditional Yoruba religion and culture in the Diaspora. Although, in this instance, the connections are intellectual rather than distinctly hereditary, as is the case in, say Bahia or Brazil. Most importantly, Oyotunji

"A Time of Destiny": Celebrating Ifa in Oyotunji

is the only African cultural community in the New World that has no links to survivals of slave cultures. Thus, in my view, it [is unique, for it] completes the African cognitive and cultural circle in the Diaspora.[22]

While the festival brought to the fore the essence of Ifa through the "time of destiny" theme, the convention gave the Oba and the Alaagba the forum necessary to elaborate on the theme and reiterate their message. As revivifiers of the Yoruba Traditional Religion, they extolled the benefits, pageantry and past glories in the African past on that fourth of July weekend in the American South. Their purpose seems to have been, in large measure, to have the uninitiated become aware of their cultural losses and accept as their destiny the challenge of reclaiming, revitalizing and promoting Ifa and Yoruba, as well as other African Traditional Religions. There was much from the Ifa Festival at Oyotunji for comparison to the Ifa Festival and culture at Ile-Ife.

Chapter 5

Notes

1. William Bascom, *Ifa Divination: Communication Between Gods and Men in West Africa* (Bloomington: Indiana University Press, 1991), 96-99.

    During the July 4th weekend, Oba Oseijeman discussed "Odu" and what is being charged for it in the United States in the Jewish and Latino communities in the video, "Egungun," a videotape in Oyotunji Village's Great Benin Films Series, 1992; this video is in the writer's possession.

2. Refer to Chapter II above on Ifa in Ile-Ife.

3. An videotape of the reading in that divination is in the writer's possession, and the author is among those babalawos recorded while reading Odu Ifa.

4. This is so basic to the African character that it hardly needs documenting, nevertheless it is discussed in by Peter J. Paris in The Spirituality of African Peoples (Minneapolis: Fortress Press, 1995), 55 for example. Refer to video footage for excerpts from this speech.

5. Documented in the videotape, *Egungun*.

6. Information from discussions with members of the Egungun Society in Ile-Ife during field study in 1992.

7. Refer to Abimbola's *Sixteen Great Poems of Ifa* (UNESCO: 1975), 259: n. 18, 19, 20. A copy of the myth is in the possession of the writer.

    Wande Abimbola explains the word "Iyami" as follows: "This is a popular name for the Yoruba witches also known as aje. This name literally means "my mother." People use the name iyami for the witches in order to avoid the use of the word aje which is believed to be too plain a reference to them."

8. This statement if quite clearly made in the video.

9. This point on the autochthones' being self-propelled is taken from Oba Oseijeman's extended talk which came later on Saturday. Refer to the *Egungun* video.

10. The Alaagba's comments are taken from the videotape, *Egungun* and are summarized and paraphrased above.

11. Ibid.

12. For more on this concept, refer to Barbara Myerhoff, "Rites of Passage: Process and Paradox," in *Celebration Studies in Festivity and Ritual*, eds., Barbara Meyerhoff and Roger

Abrahamson (Washington, D.C.: Smithsonian Institution Press, 1982), 118.

13. This information is taken rom the author's videotape archive.
14. Based on the author's observations.
15. Refer to the *Egungun* videotape that is summarized and paraphrased for the reader's convenience.
16. Taken from video footage of the 1992 Ifa Festival in Oyotunji, as is also in the essay, "Verbal Performance as Art," 4-5.
17. Ibid.
18. Ibid.
19. The paper on "Coconut Theology" was read by a pastor from Tonga during the First Pan-African Christian Church Conference at the Interdenominational Theological Center (ITC), Atlanta, which I attended in 1988. Audiotape of paper is in the author's possession.
20. Oba Oseijeman, "Keynote Address," 3, a pamphlet in the author's possession.
21. Medahochi had this publication in his possession and read directly from it; it should be recoverable archives housing African Americana.
22. "Completing the Circle: Notes on African Art, Society, and Religion in Oyotunji, South Carolina," *African Arts* 24, No. 3 (July 1991), 66-79.

Afterword

This study has offered a comparative study of Ifa Festivals in Ile-Ife, Nigeria, and Oyotunji African Village in Sheldon, South Carolina. The time-span (from the primal, pre-Oduduwa era to post-modernity) and the cross-religious dimensions (Ile-Ife-Yoruba and African American-New Yoruba) of this study necessitated that I employ a long historical view methodology and a cross-cultural analysis. In addition, I have utilized the lenses of other disciplines, primarily including religion but also ethnology and literature.

I described the Ifa canon and conventions—as aspects of Yoruba traditional culture—and the 1992 Ifa Festivals, with attention to cultural continuity and textual redaction. The central question on which this study focused was how much are Ifa Festivals and traditions in Oyotunji like those in Ile-Ife? Although Oyotunji's Ifa Festival and associated activities do not adhere strictly to the Ile-Ife model, the two communities are remarkably similar in their utilization and celebration of Ifa tradition in the contemporary world.

IFA RELIGION

One of the most important of these similarities is that of what the Yoruba of Ile-Ife and the New Yoruba of Oyotunji think of Ifa. Ifa adherents understand Ifa to be a divining system that has a corresponding canonical literature. They believe that the wisdom of Ifa can be accessed by Ifa priests/babalawos/Iyalawos who have passed through major aspects of the ancient rites of initiation. This rite certifies that the initiate has a practicing knowledge of the Ifa literary corpus and is trained to divine principally with *ikin* and the *opele* chain. Ifa divination functions as the method by which the Supreme Being's wisdom and knowledge, usually indirectly through the orishas, is made known to mortals. The babalawos/iyalawos are the conduits through which messages from the divine are channeled to the client. The Yoruba Traditional Religion is mediated and preserved through Ifa divination, which the Annual Ifa Festivals celebrate.

Like the Ile-Ife Yoruba—and Yorubas elsewhere in the world, the people of Oyotunji think of Ifa as having practical purpose in their daily lives. Literally every aspect of Yoruba traditional life is touched by Ifa, including cosmological thought, historical perspective, political organization, family and other social structures, the major rites of passages in life, individual behavior and accomplishment, matters of health and healing, to list a few. Actually, Ifa is consulted on all matters and particularly whenever there are important decisions to be made. This pervasiveness in individual and corporate lives is so widespread and of such depth that the Yoruba Traditional Religion and Ifa are interdependent.

Reflected within the Odu Ifa is the Yoruba Traditional understanding of ultimate reality as a cosmic construct from which all life and structures in the universe originated. The sense of destiny—the setting of the universe and its unfolding history—in the cosmos is central to the New Yoruba cosmology as well. Central to the Yoruba worldview is the belief that every human has a destiny discernable via Ifa divination. The course of destiny for an individual or corporate entity is discernible as energy and may need to be readjusted periodically for harmony. Divination reassures the client that s/he is on the proper course or road to move harmoniously through life. Ifa religious festivals in Ile-Ife and Oyotunji illuminate the centrality of Ifa divination with respect to individual and communal destinies. This illumination for insight into destinies is what is celebrated in Ifa Festivals.

CONTINUITY AND CHANGE

Yoruba religion and culture in Ile-Ife have been impacted by outside influences. Ifa worshippers in Ile-Ife seem to have been impacted by two worlds—the traditional Muslims and migrating Africans and the Christians. Whether aspects of Ifa divination have Muslim origins is an issue seldom debated and mostly settled in favor of an Ile-Ife provenance. The emergence of patriarchy in Ile-Ife during the era of Islamic invasions of Africa suggests a Muslim influence on that kingdom's religious, social, and cultural life. Sexist elements were exacerbated during the era of British patriarchal rule, and some redactions in the Ifa canon may have derived from Christianity. The architectural design of the Ifa Temple is certain to have been inspired by the presence and practices of Christian missionaries. Although the modern Ifa priests use Christian-era, linear time to schedule activities, their Ifa Festival still is ritually tied to natural cyclings of agriculture. The Ifa Festival celebrates the arrival of the first harvest—that of the yam and commemorates Elysian days. The Ifa priesthood's capitulation to change is tempered by their devotion to continuity. The interpretational dynamic within the Ifa canon and Yoruba culture permit incremental changes.

Ifa divination and other sacred rituals suggest that they are a remnant of a tradition that is indigenous and traceable back to a primal era in Ile-Ife. Because of its likely antiquity and diminished appeal following the spread of Christianity and Islam among the Yoruba, Traditionalists perceive Ifa Religion to be anachronistic yet practical. After the British left, the Ifa Traditionalists began a revitalization movement in order to cast a positive image on the religion while removing the tarnish from decades of colonial denigration of the divination system and its priesthood.

Some of the iyalawos/babalawos took steps to make Ifa religion more appealing by organizing Ijo Orunmila, which identifies with aspects of the Christian Church. Iyalawo/babalawo members of Ijo Orunmila say, for example, that the canonical Odu Ifa is equivalent with the Bible. Ijo Orunmila also emphasizes the worship of Olodumare as Supreme Being along with the orishas, giving an implicit nod to monotheism. In-depth treatment of the recasting of Ifa Religion is a subject for another manuscript.

Oyotunji reclaimed this traditional religion in the 1960s and 1970s as part of the African American cultural nationalist movement. The Oyotunji Movement evolved out of the African American desire to reject oppressive Christian and political traditions that were moderated by race. They embraced African traditional cultures from which their ancestors had been detached during slavery. Thus, Oyotunji's revival of Ifa the religious tradition is a more than twenty-five-year-old African American Movement. Oba Oseijeman began to construct the Oyotunji Movement under other organizational names and with a more cultural nationalist emphasis in New York City, later relocating it to the South.

Afterword

In contrast to the Ile-Ife Ifa religious tradition, the New Yoruba of Oyotunji are careful to screen from public display the controversial activities of the festival. They exhibit virtually no divination or healing during public activities. They also are careful not to allow carcasses from animal and other blood sacrifices to be placed for open view after such a ceremony. Because of their diasporic experiences, the New Yoruba have sought to continue Ifa religious tradition but with innovative sensitivity to Western sensibilities.

Although there is no Christian edifice in Oyotunji, the New Yoruba do realize that African American culture was formed within a Christian context and that a number of folk among them are former Christians. A few still attend Christian churches periodically. Therefore, Oba Oseijeman has been meticulous in trying to weed out Catholicism and other Christian aspects from direct association with his movement. Yet, it may be that as former Christians (with a few former Black Muslims and Muslim sympathizers), the New Yoruba undoubtedly can identify with Ifa religious tradition because aspects of African religion bear resemblance to Christianity. There are, for example, proverbs, miracle narratives, and mythological deities as well as rituals of sacrifice, dying and resurrection in both Old and New Testament and Ifa cannons.

The strength of Ifa religious tradition is in the adaptability (redactability) of its (orature/scripture) literary corpus, for this has allowed the religion to endure. On the other hand, the redactability of images in the literature of the Ifa Odu was conducive to the kind of tampering that transformed Ifa religious tradition, allowing it to be patriarchal rather than based on the indigenous, more mother's rights. Unfortunately, the New Yorubas have adopted, though with some moderation, the sexism that is a hallmark of the Yoruba culture and Ifa traditions.

The New Yorubas were not born into Ifa traditional religions, so they have had to adopt African names and cultivate new identities. They built a "homeland." Their village concept has been reconstructed from books and based on observations during visits to Ile-Ife, Oyo, Abeokuta and other Yoruba towns and states. It is remarkable that, from the distance of their trans-Atlantic and nearly four-hundred year old diasporic view, the New Yorubas have reconstructed a village and traditional religion that are recognized as authentic by nearly anyone familiar with Yoruba tradition.

Oyotunji instituted a reformulation of Ife's redacted Ifa tradition. It is a religious and cultural entity organized with the intention of being an antidote to racism and ravages of capitalism in the United States. To this extent Oyotunji African Village represents a black cultural nationalist movement, which believes it has the prophetic mission of calling African Americans to return to their African heritages and especially to Ifa.

Ile-Ife has a mixed population, consisting of Yoruba Christians and Muslims and persons from the diverse Yoruba ethnic groups. There also are Igbo, Efik, and Bini of eastern Nigeria and peoples from other parts of Nigeria as well as folks from other African countries, the Diaspora and Europe. In Oyotunji African Americans and their children predominate. In this respect, Oyotunji may be more like the autochthonous village of like-minded settlers—Ifa worshipers and supporters—than like contemporary Ile-Ife that coexists with ethnic and religious diversity. There is, however, an area of Ile-Ife that is identified with a pre-Oduduwa, primal populace.

While Yoruba religion and Ifa divination is considered by priests to be a transformation of its autochthonous beginnings, in Oyotunji Yoruba religion is mixed with Fa of Dahomey, for example, and therefore is eclectic. The New Yoruba have consciously utilized elements from outside Ifa in initiation rituals, for example, whereas the transformations and redactions in the Ifa cannon may be described as evolutionary and not conscious borrowings in the present from other African religious traditions. The New Yoruba appear to borrow in order to accommodate varied interests of African Americans who travel to Africa and see religious tradtions in action or read about them and want to be initiated into a non-Yoruba but African priesthood. Oyotunji appears to be more inclined to appeal to the best judgment of African Americans and to be subject to appealing to the African Americans to see the usefulness of Ifa Religion and divination and how it can be applied to enrich their lives. Since most African Americans have no idea of the ethnic group from which their ancestors originated in West Africa, they choose the group whose culture or religious tradition they would like to practice, with the exception of those like the Oba of Oyotunji who was introduced to the Ifa religious system through a Santeria initiation in Cuba.

Oyotunji has not written odu to recount its version of creation or recreation in North America and continues to draw from Ile-Ife's narratives. Although the Ile-Ife Ifa worshipers are aware of redactions in the literary images in the Ifa sacred narratives, Oyotunji necessarily expends its energies trying to reconstruct Ifa religious tradition and other aspects of Yoruba culture. Therefore, Oyotunji tends to accept images as they find them from one part of the narratives to another, too often referring to them more as dualities rather than understanding them to be historical changes within the sacred literature. The consensus that there should be no autonomous, female-Ifa priests is an example of Oyotunji's tendency to borrow from contemporary Ile-Ife priestly conduct rather than consider the extent to which aspects of their borrowings are based on redacted religious texts and transformed Yoruba culture.

With Oyotunji better established, the next generations undoubtedly will expend more time asking more questions of a historical nature. Successive generations of New Yorubas may consciously decide whether to reconstruct the village along more autochthonous (pre-Oduduwa) lines (that may be more in tune with modernity) rather than repeat conventions of the Oduduwa conquest. At that point Oyotunji may lead Ile-Ife's Ifa priesthood beyond the confines of patriarchy and Oduduwa conventions.

There may always have been three-dimensional objects and images in Yoruba Traditional Religion. Nevertheless, the New Yorubas felt the need to make the religion more visual for African Americans who only recently were introduced to Ifa. The New Yorubas added a multiplicity of images and symbols of orishas. Thus, visual arts such as painted murals, advertisement banners, photographs, art deco, and print and electronic audio-visual materials were devised to ancient orature and cryptographed formulations. The visual arts are represented in priestly objects and orisa emblems and images created by Oba Oseijeman, the late Chief Awolowo, and Medahochi, in particular.

Afterword

CLOSING COMMENT

Oyotunji represents a valiant attempt to reclaim aspects of Africa by patterning itself after redacted, religious tradition in Ile-Ife. The Oba and African American researchers adopted and improvised religion and culture as they (re)discovered it in books in the 1960s and 1970s. The redacted aspects of the Ifa traditions in Ile-Ife are as pertinent to gender relations and nationalistic goals in Oyotunji as to theological meanings.

Oyotunji is a religio-cultural movement within the United States that has a two-fold goal, which is both negative and positive. In a resistance stance, the New Yorubas intend to disparage Christianity and repudiate the conventional African American identity. The New Yorubas have assumed an African identity and tried to recover African—though principally Yoruba—traditional values. They promote awareness and hope to extend the scope of the movement among African Americans by promoting Oyotunji as a hedge against ravages of social and economic discrimination against Blacks in the United States.

THE IFA FESTIVAL

The Annual Ifa Festival of 1992 was Oyotunji's twentieth. This celebration is of such antiquity in Ile-Ife that the festivals are not counted linearly as calendar-based anniversaries are. Ifa religious tradition grew out of the soil with the people and their institutions in Ile-Ife; it became associated with the city-state's agrarian cycles. That association has been symbolized in the dynamics between the priesthood of Ifa and the Ooni who is titular head of the Ile-Ife Yoruba.

Although the public aspects of the Ifa Religious Festival in Oyotunji were consistent with the spirit of the festival in Ile-Ife, there were aspects that clearly were innovations, i. e. the Elegba dance, the egungun, and apetibi dances. I found them to be informative and appropriate, and I believe the New Yorubas displayed these innovations in order to share with the public the pageantry and ritual of Yoruba culture as it relates to Ifa religious tradition. The three rituals are of precisely the kind that African Americans would find exotically interesting and those about which they would be likely to know nothing unless they have seen them in museum exhibitions or read about them. These rituals provide a dramatic way to call attention to how much African religious traditions the African descendants in the United States lost while displaying aspects of Ifa religious traditions.

An interesting contrast between Ile-Ife and Oyotunji is seen in the roles played by the heads of religious institutions. The Ooni does not fully participant in Ebgodo Ooni. Oba Oseijeman's role seems more akin to that of a priest-king, which apparently was the role of the pre-Oduduwa Ooni. In Oyotunji, therefore, the priesthood is elevated rather than subjugated to the political power of the titular head of the Yoruba People in Ile-Ife, where the subjugation continues to this day.

One of the least traditionally attractive activities in the Ifa religious festival at Oyotunji is Ile-Ife's most appealing. That activity is the verbal art or recitation/reading aloud the Holy Odu or Scripture of Ifa. In the festival at Ile-Ife, this activity is highly animated with a great deal of call/response from iyalawos/babalawos who speak Yoruba. In Oyotunji, this period of activity took on the aura of a performance-watched-by-spectators. No small part of the aura derived from the clumsiness of Oyotunji Ifa priests who tried to read and recite Ifa texts. Here

Afterword

the lack of proficiency of virtually every priest, with the exception of the Oba, Medahochi, and one or two other chiefs, is obvious. But these New Yoruba Ifa priests have had little training in Ifa priestly languages. At least one Ifa priest in Ile-Ife recited odu in English during the festival at Ile-Ife; he apparently had greater facility in English than in Yoruba. Having made the point, I hasten to say the recitations from Ifa texts are known to have archaic words and phrases that are difficult for even the Yoruba-bred Ifa priests to master. Despite the roughness of the reciting and reading, the verbal display of Odu Ifa gave some of Oyotunji's Ifa priests the opportunity to practice their skills in reciting and/or reading in the Yoruba language. During that period, they listened also to others interpret the meanings of the Ifa verses and acquired enhanced familiarity with the Ifa literary texts.

The time may come when the priests of Ifa in Oyotunji will indigenize the language and other aspects of Ifa Tradition so that it is more conducive to African American interests and concerns, for the subject already has surfaced in Ifa Festival discourse. Oyotunji's existence within the capitalistic United States affords no one the leisure of dedicating his life entirely to the study and practice of Ifa Tradition; these folk have to give attention to earning a living at tasks outside the movement that produce adequate incomes for maintenance within a currency-based society. But neither do the Ifa priests in Ile-Ife, including the Awoni, have the leisure of traditional times to expend on Ifa celebrations and rituals.

Despite self-consciousness among Ifa Traditionalists, they are not too shy to carry out prescribed Ifa rituals during public ceremonies. At the Ifa Festival, e. g., the Awoni mixed salves and invited on-lookers to apply the healing ointments to their bodies. They marked the Odu in iyerosun and encouraged the guests to ingest the refined wood particles, passing the crytogram around for on-lookers to partake of. These priests sacrificed, and left for display in the temple, a goat. They publicly displayed their devotion to the deity Ifa and other orisa and ancestors, as well as to Olodumare.

ON WOMEN AND THE IFA PRIESTHOOD

This study has shown that there is a potential within Ifa tradition for maintaining the status quo, but there is also a revolutionizing principle. Both energies are expressed in Ile-Ife and in Oyotunji. Ifa has been used in reactionary ways to bring about the devolution of women's roles and privileges within the Ifa priesthood. This devolution was indicative of pre-festival rituals and some of the roles of the participating principals. The recitations from Ifa texts and the authority of the priesthood help perpetuate sexist thinking and behavior toward women.

In both Ile-Ife and Oyotunji, women who know the sacred art and sciences of Ifa divination and its associated literary texts do command a presence. They frequently do much of the hard work associated with initiations to Ifa and may be highly sought after Ifa diviners. Women have yet, however, to acquire the privilege of full initiation into the Ifa priesthood. Moreover, they have no self-autonomy within that body, a status that women seem to have been deprived of after the onset of the Oduduwa dynasty. In Ile-Ife, Ifa and other orishas are worshipped without interference or hassle from the state and are honored by many citizens.

The Yoruba's Ifa is marginalized as counter-cultural in the United States. Yet, the Oyotunji movement has inscripted some of the sexist attitudes and practices of the Ile-Ife priesthood. This is so, no doubt, because the priesthood in Oyotunji did not pursue historical investigation of redactions in the Ifa canon. Pressure from women (iyalawos and apetibis) who do so much of the work for initiations and other ceremonies within the movement may be having an ameliorating effect on this front. This is indicated by the 1993 Oyotunji trip to the Republic of Benin for both female and male initiations into the Fa priesthood. In gatherings subsequent to the 1992 Festival, residents of Oyotunji discussed their travel. The Republic of Benin was a reasonable target considering the relatively more conscious memory among those priests of a connection between the Fa system and a female Supreme Being and a chief female deity of divination.

The comparative study of Ifa Festivals in Ile-Ife and Oyotunji may lead to a more comprehensive understanding of Ifa Tradition generally. The more we study Ifa religious tradition and festivals in Oyotunji, and no doubt also in other parts of the Diaspora, the more insight we will be afforded into traditional religions and cultures in Africa and in the Diaspora.

Photos

Stone slab said to be Ifa's footprint

The Agbonbon inside the Ifa Temple Prior to the Festival in Ile-Ife

Ifa priests divine in the Temple in Ile-Ife during the Ifa Festival program

Photos

The Iyalodu gives a Stirring Speech During the Festival Program in the Ifa Temple

Aseda and neice during his House's Awoni Festival

Offering to Ifa from the Aseda's House during the Awoni Festival

Entrance to Oyotunji Village bearing sketches of horsemen with a rifle and a spear, a metaphor of Old Oyo

Photos

Egungun masqueraders in palace courtyard in Oyotunji

Yemonja Temple on the Ifa Festival Pilgrimage

Oba Oseijeman and other babalawos gather in palace courtyard to recite Ifa verses

Appendix

"THE FIRST ATTEMPT TO ESTABLISH A LIVING ON EARTH"

From *IFISM: The Complete Work of Orunmila* (Efehi Ltd., Lagos, Nigeria, 1986), 14-19

God evolved a plan for dispatching all the divinities to earth simultaneously but without any advance warning. One fine morning therefore, God called on his maid Arugba to invite each of the divinities from their respective homes to appear at the Heavenly Palace the following morning for a special assignment.

Arugba set out very early that morning. However before then, God had prepared a special chamber completely equipped with various implements with which He expected the divinities to carry out their assignments on earth. Arugba's message to each . . . was clear. "My Father has sent me to invite you to prepare for a special assignment tomorrow morning. You are to get your self prepared to set out for the assignment as soon as the divine message is given to you. You are not to return to your house before embarking on the mission."

Most of the divinities took the message literally. . . . Arugba visited the houses of the divinities in order of seniority, which meant that Orunmila, the most junior ... was the last to be visited.

Meanwhile, Orunmila who was in the habit of making a situation divination every morning, was advised by Ifa to make a feast on that particular day in anticipation of all callers to his residence. At the time that Arugba got to Orunmila's house, it was already very late in the evening. Not having taken any meal since morning, Arugba was already very hungry when she got to Orunmila's house. Before allowing her to deliver the divine message, Orunmila persuaded her to have meal. She ate to her satisfaction and then told Orunmila that God wanted him to report to His palace the next day, together with the other divinities for a special errand.

In appreciation of Orunmila's hospitality, she confided further in him by disclosing the details of the errand that God had in store for them. She advised him to ask for three special favours from God in addition to whatever instruments he would collect from God's inner-chamber for his mission. He was to ask for the Camelion, ... the multi-coloured hen [,] ... and God's own special bag... In a final aside, Arugba told Orunmila that if he so desired he could also persuade God to let her accompany him on his mission. With words of advice Arugba left for home, having completed her assignment.

The following morning, ... all the divinities reported.... As soon as they got there, God ordered each of them to proceed on the journey to earth without returning to their respective homes.... The first divinities to get to the earth soon discovered that there was no ground there to tread upon. The whole place was still waterlogged. There was only one palm-tree which stood in the middle of the water with its roots in heaven, ... As they were coming in, they had no where else to stay except on the branches of the palm-tree. It was a very hard time indeed.

Before leaving heaven, each of the divinities collected from God's inner chamber all the materials and instruments of their choice. It is the same instruments that iniates to the cults of each divinity use for initiation to this day.

By the time Orunmila came to the Palace of God, all the others had gone.... He was told like the others, to collect whatever instruments he found in the inner chamber. However, all the available instruments had at that time been collected by the others and since there was only one empty Snail's shell left, he had no choice but to hold on to it. He then appealed to God that since he had nothing to collect from the inner Chamber, he should be given:

a. The Camelion—the oldest creature in the house of God to advise him on how to tackle the teething problems of terrestrial habitation;
b. The multi-coloured hen;
c. The Almighty Father's own Divine Bag, to collect things he was going with; and,
d. The privilege of going to earth with Arugba, to remind them of the rules of heaven.

His four wishes were granted. As he was leaving, he collected four different plants, which Ifa priests use for all their preparations to this day. He also collected a sample of the plants and animals that he could lay hands upon.

He kept all his collections inside the bag....

When Orunmila reached the gateway to earth, he found all the other divinities hanging on to the palm-tree branches. He too had no option but to join them.

After Orunmila had been sitting or standing on the palm-tree branch for some time, Arugba advised him from within the Divine Bag, where she was kept, to turn the mouth of the smail's shell downwards into the water below because it contained the foundation soil of the earth which would make the ground hard for treading on. Orunmila who had collected the empty snail's shell from the inner chamber of God did not know its contents.... All the other ... [divinities] had ignored it. None of them except Arugba knew that it contained the Secret of the Earth.

Heaps of sand ... started piling up around the foot of the palm-tree. After so many heaps had formed, Arubga once again spoke to Orunmila from within the bag, this time, advising him to drop the hen down to the heaps of sand. As it scattered the heaps, the area of the ground began to spread.... [Scratching] is the same operation that the hen is still performing to this day.

After the grounds had been extended over a large area, the other divinities who were now amazed at the mysterious performance of Orunmila ordered him to go down and tread on the ground to verify whether it could support them.

Once again, Arugba advised Orunmila from within the bag, to drop the Camelion to tread first on the ground. The Camelion walked about stealthily on the ground, for fear it would collapse under its feet. But the ground held together, and it is the same cautious walking process to which the Camelion ... [is] accustomed to this day....

As soon as Orunmila was sure that the ground was strong enough, he came down to earth from the palm-tree branch and his first task was to transplant the plants he brought from heaven. Thereafter, all the other divinities came down to earth one after the other.

That is why the palm-tree [,] the first creation . . . which had its roots from heaven, is respected by all the divinities. It is the root of their genealogy. All the divinities spread out from the palm-tree to establish their various abodes in different parts of the earth.

Orunmila, being the youngest, . . . stayed with and served each of the more elderly ones in turn. He served Ogun, Sango, Olokun, Eziza etc. In the course of his servitude, one of the divinities seized Arugba from him. . . . [Orunmila] was thus deprived of his chief counsel and confidant. . .

The woman who carries the iken [sic] on her head to UGBODU is called Arugba. . . .

The presence of Arugba as the only woman. . . created a host of problems for the divinities. One after the other, they fought to retain her. The struggle for Arugba soon brought out the worst in the divinities. . . . There was complete confusion which led to acrimony among them. This time, Orunmila was the first to return to heaven to make a report to God. The guardian role of Arugba became lost to the divinities because she had been deprived of the company of Orunmila with whom she came to the world. . . .

Orunmila had lost the use of all the things he brought including even the Divine Bag which without the advise of Arugba, he did not know how to use. . . .

One after the other, they all trooped back to heaven to report mission impossible. They also decided that they were going to request God to give them Divine authority (ashe) with which they could cause things to happen, for mortal servants to serve them and for money with which to do business with one another....

God gave it to all of them.... All of them including Orunmila were ordered to return to earth to complete the mission they had started.

After the male orishas went to heaven to complain about the conflicts among them, a number of misfortunes and adversities—including money, greed, and death—came to earth with their return. Just after Orunmila acquired control over all of the other divinities, Ifa came to advise Orunmila, apparently in the absence of Arugba. Although there is no mention of what finally happened to Arugba, the narrative does suggest that the male divinities did not have enough ashe among them without Arugba to avoid a flooding of the earth and their second transfiguration to heaven. Could it be that this commentary provides a feminist twist on the narrative that seemed to Djisovi and me to be straightforward in its story line? Our analysis led us to believe that historical markers that are imbedded in narratives such as this could be used effectively to read correctives into Yoruba history and bring equity for women in Ifa culture and Yoruba society.

Index

Abesan / Oya 18, 19, 22
Adelade 17, 18
Adjakata / Hevioso 22, 25, 31, 92, 99
African Soul Brothers 10, 12-16, 21
Alaagba 21, 87, 97, 142-145, 147, 157
Apetibi 66, 151, 169
Araba 58, 112, 114, 117, 119-123, 129, 142
Ashe 102, 184, 185
Awoni 5, 26, 29, 38, 57-59, 61, 111-123, 125, 126, 128, 136, 147, 170, 176, 177

Baba Oseijeman / Oba Oseijeman 17-19, 23, 27, 30, 32, 38, 74, 82, 83, 85 – 87, 92-94, 97, 98, 141, 144, 148, 149, 151, 164, 167, 179
Babalawo 7, 38, 53, 55, 56, 58, 66, 67, 85, 89, 101, 111, 113, 115, 116, 123, 127, 128, 139, 141, 142, 152, 155, 163

Babatunde Olatunji 23, 120, 131
Bokonon 25, 103
Brays Island Road 21, 86-88
Chief (Akinyele) Elemosha Awolowo 21, 29, 52, 85, 86, 115, 122, 125, 167
Chief (Shangodele) Medahochi Omowale Zannu 27
Chief Akintobe 87
Chief Edubi Ajamu 87
Chief Eleshin 87
Chief Olofundeyi Olaitan 142

Drum Majors for Justice Committee 14

Egbe Egun / Egungun 21, 24, 62, 90, 97, 131, 132, 142-146, 150, 169, 178
Egungun 'La 142, 144, 145
Elegba/Esu 8, 22, 53, 83, 90, 114, 127, 141

Fa Du 92, 99, 150

Fon 9, 24, 82, 91-93, 98, 99, 149

Ibo: Ikin Divination device 8
Ifa 3-11, 13, 15-21, 23-31, 33, 37-67, 73-75, 77, 79, 81, 83, 85, 87, 89-93, 95, 97, 99-105, 109-137, 139-157, 160-172, 175-179, 181, 182, 185
Ifa Festival Songs 22, 23, 47, 51, 52, 95, 96, 118, 120, 124, 131-135, 143, 149, 151-153
Ifa Festival at Ile-Ife / *Odun ifa* 126
Ifa Festival at Oyotunji 157
Ijo Orunmila 28, 47, 95, 116, 123, 163
Ikin Divination 49
Ikukomi / Oloye Atokun Eegun 130, 131
Ile-Ife 3, 5, 7, 23-30, 37-46, 51, 57-59, 61, 62, 66, 67, 74, 84, 88, 89, 98, 102-104, 109-111, 113-115, 117-119, 121-127, 129-131, 133, 135-137, 139, 140, 142-149, 153-157, 160-172, 175
Irunmoles 40, 123, 125, 132
Islam / *Odu Otua Meji* 44, 77, 102, 163
Iya Ato 143
Iya Orite 151
Iyalodu Agbyeawo Ooni-Ile-Ife 122, 176
Iyanifa 7, 26, 66, 102, 116, 127

King, Walter / Oba Oseijeman 27, 30, 32, 38, 74, 92-94, 97, 98, 141, 144, 148, 149, 151, 164, 167, 179
Kpojito Omiyale Hwesihuno 21

Mama Keke 83
Merindinlogun 7, 17, 60, 63, 83, 85, 100, 122

Obatala 40-42, 45, 66, 74, 86, 90, 117-119, 141, 152, 153
Odu Ifa 6-8, 17-19, 26, 28, 40, 49, 50, 56, 61, 62, 67, 92, 102, 120, 124, 127, 133, 149, 151, 152, 161, 170
Odu Ogbe-Rosun 125
Odu: Female Assistant to Olodumare 6-8, 17-19, 26-28, 40, 42, 44, 45, 49-51, 54-56, 58-65, 67, 92, 95, 99, 101, 102, 120, 123-125, 127, 128, 133, 144, 149, 151-153, 161, 163, 164, 166, 169-171
Oduduwa 37, 39-45, 47, 49, 51, 53, 55, 57-61, 63, 65-67, 84, 111, 117-119, 160, 166, 167, 169, 171
Olodu 58, 63, 127, 128, 151
Olodumare 6, 19, 39, 41, 42, 51, 59-61, 64, 148, 163, 171
Olubunmi Omi Tonade 86

Index

Oluwo 29, 56, 111, 126, 129
Omilade Zannu 86, 87, 91
Ooni 23, 29, 39, 57, 58, 66, 89, 111, 112, 114-116, 119, 122, 125-127, 129, 131, 147, 168, 169
Opele Chain Divination 8, 66, 90, 161
Opon Ifa 8
Ori 17, 152
Orisha / Orisa 4, 5, 8, 18, 19, 21-23, 25, 40, 41, 47, 51, 53, 61, 67, 73, 74, 79, 83, 85, 86, 90, 91, 93, 97-99, 104, 111, 114, 149, 156, 167, 171
Osaara / *Odun Agbon* 111, 112, 121
Oshun 60-62, 64, 67, 90, 101, 102, 117, 122, 151
Oyotunji African Village 3, 5, 98

Paige's Point, South Carolina 22, 85, 86
Predestination 52, 53

Santeria 17, 78-80, 82, 83, 86, 93, 104, 156, 166
Sheldon, South Carolina 3, 5, 32, 74, 87, 149, 160
Smalls, Robert and Belle 86

Tosu Tosasalem 92
Tyehimba 24

Vodun 25, 93, 98, 156

Women and the Ifa Priesthood 171

Yoruba 3-10, 16-18, 21, 22, 24-30, 37-40, 42-45, 47-49, 51, 53, 56-58, 61-65, 67, 73, 74, 79-88, 90, 91, 93-100, 102-104, 109, 111, 112, 115-117, 119-121, 126, 131-133, 136, 141, 142, 144-148, 150-152, 155-157, 160-170, 185

171208-1-200-60W